I0438626

Modeling Flood Plain Hydrology and Forest Productivity of Congaree Swamp, South Carolina

By Thomas W. Doyle

Prepared in cooperation with the National Park Service

Scientific Investigations Report 2009–5130

U.S. Department of the Interior
U.S. Geological Survey

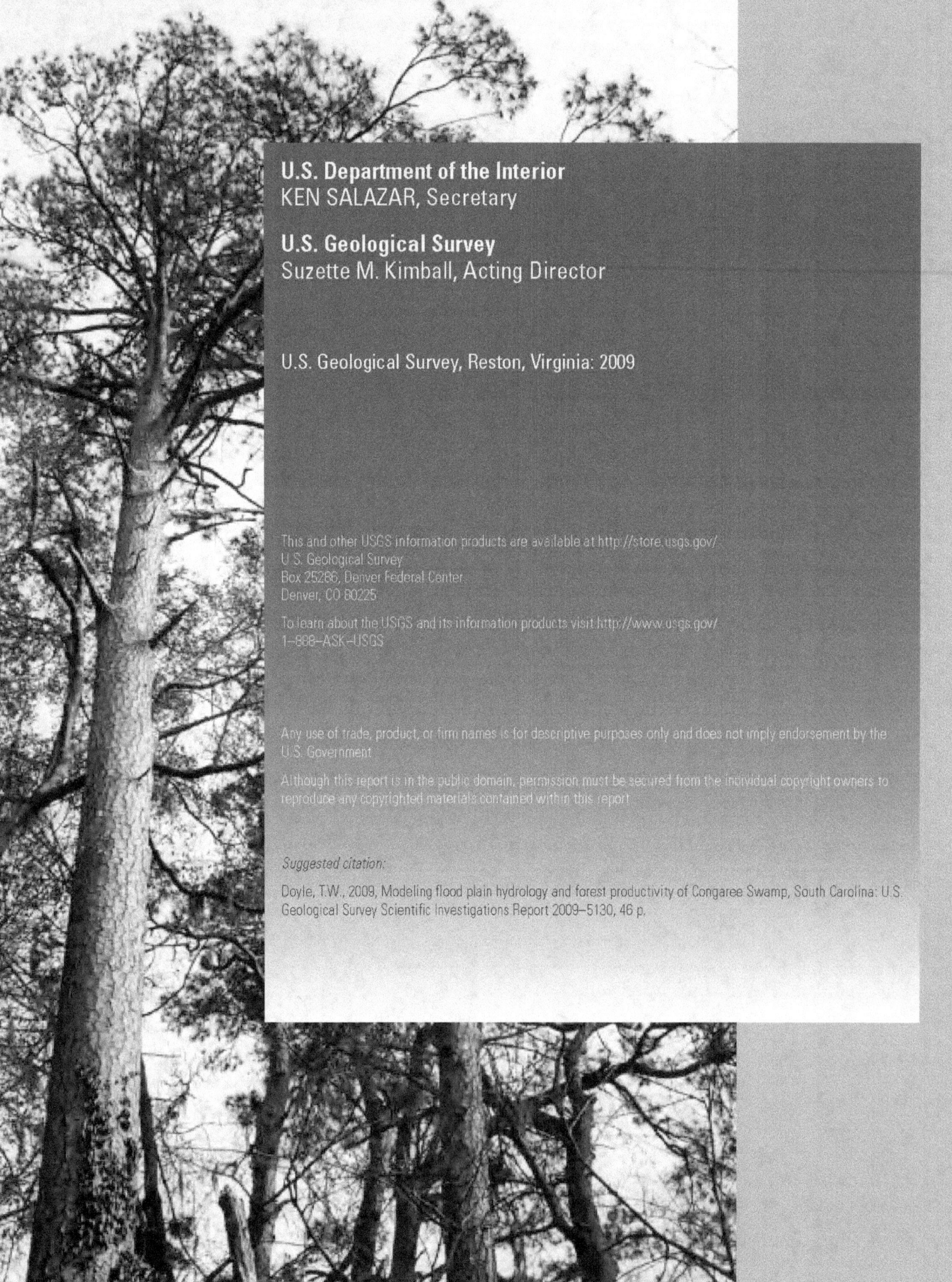

U.S. Department of the Interior
KEN SALAZAR, Secretary

U.S. Geological Survey
Suzette M. Kimball, Acting Director

U.S. Geological Survey, Reston, Virginia: 2009

This and other USGS information products are available at http://store.usgs.gov/
U.S. Geological Survey
Box 25286, Denver Federal Center
Denver, CO 80225

To learn about the USGS and its information products visit http://www.usgs.gov/
1-888-ASK-USGS

Suggested citation:

Doyle, T.W., 2009, Modeling flood plain hydrology and forest productivity of Congaree Swamp, South Carolina: U.S. Geological Survey Scientific Investigations Report 2009–5130, 46 p.

Contents

Figures

Tables

Conversion Factors and Datums

Multiply	By	To obtain
Length		
centimeter (cm)	0.3937	inch (in.)
millimeter (mm)	0.03937	inch (in.)
meter (m)	3.281	foot (ft)
kilometer (km)	0.6214	mile (mi)
meter (m)	1.094	yard (yd)
Area		
hectare (ha)	2.471	acre
square kilometer (km^2)	247.1	acre
square centimeter (cm^2)	0.001076	square foot (ft^2)
square centimeter (cm^2)	0.1550	square inch (ft^2)
hectare (ha)	0.003861	square mile (mi^2)
square kilometer (km^2)	0.3861	square mile (mi^2)
Flow rate		
meter per second (m/s)	3.281	foot per second (ft/s)

Temperature in degrees Celsius (°C) can be converted to degrees Fahrenheit (°F) as follows:

$$°F = (1.8 \times °C) + 32$$

Vertical coordinate information is referenced to the North American Vertical Datum of 1988 (NAVD 88).

Horizontal coordinate information is referenced to the North American Datum of 1983 (NAD 83).

Modeling Flood Plain Hydrology and Forest Productivity of Congaree Swamp, South Carolina

By Thomas W. Doyle

Abstract

An ecological field and modeling study was conducted to examine the flood relations of backswamp forests and park trails of the flood plain portion of Congaree National Park, S.C. Continuous water level gages were distributed across the length and width of the flood plain portion—referred to as "Congaree Swamp"—to facilitate understanding of the lag and peak flood coupling with stage of the Congaree River. A severe and prolonged drought at study start in 2001 extended into late 2002 before backswamp zones circulated floodwaters. Water levels were monitored at 10 gaging stations over a 4-year period from 2002 to 2006. Historical water level stage and discharge data from the Congaree River were digitized from published sources and U.S. Geological Survey (USGS) archives to obtain long-term daily averages for an upstream gage at Columbia, S.C., dating back to 1892. Elevation of ground surface was surveyed for all park trails, water level gages, and additional circuits of roads and boundaries. Rectified elevation data were interpolated into a digital elevation model of the park trail system. Regression models were applied to establish time lags and stage relations between gages at Columbia, S.C., and gages in the upper, middle, and lower reaches of the river and backswamp within the park. Flood relations among backswamp gages exhibited different retention and recession behavior between flood plain reaches with greater hydroperiod in the lower reach than those in the upper and middle reaches of the Congaree Swamp. A flood plain inundation model was developed from gage relations to predict critical river stages and potential inundation of hiking trails on a real-time basis and to forecast the 24-hour flood condition on the trail network within the park.

In addition, tree-ring analysis was used to evaluate the effects of flood events and flooding history on forest resources at Congaree National Park. Tree cores were collected from populations of loblolly pine (*Pinus taeda*), baldcypress (*Taxodium distichum*), water tupelo (*Nyssa aquatica*), green ash (*Fraxinus pennslyvanica*), laurel oak (*Quercus laurifolia*), swamp chestnut oak (*Quercus michauxii*), and sycamore (*Plantanus occidentalis*) within Congaree Swamp in high- and low-elevation sites characteristic of shorter and longer flood duration and related to upriver flood controls and dam operation. Ring counts and dating indicated that all loblolly pine trees and nearly all baldcypress collections in this study are postsettlement recruits and old-growth cohorts, dating from 100 to 300 years in age. Most hardwood species and trees cored for age analysis were less than 100 years old, demonstrating robust growth and high site quality. Growth chronologies of loblolly pine and baldcypress exhibited positive and negative inflections over the last century that corresponded with climate history and residual effects of Hurricane Hugo in 1989. Stemwood production on average was less for trees and species on sites with longer flood retention and hydroperiod affected more by groundwater seepage and site elevation than river floods. Water level data provided evidence that stream regulation and operations of the Saluda Dam (post-1934) have actually increased the average daily water stage in the Congaree River. There was no difference in tree growth response by species or hydrogeomorphic setting to predam and postdam flood conditions and river stage. Climate-growth analysis showed that long-term growth variation is controlled more by spring/summer temperatures in loblolly pine and by spring/summer precipitation in baldcypress than flooding history.

Introduction

Congaree National Park was established in 1976 by congressional mandate "… to preserve and protect for the education, inspiration, and enjoyment of present and future generations an outstanding example of a near-virgin southern hardwood forest" (Public Law 94–545, 1976). The park holdings include an 8,903-ha old-growth bottomland hardwood flood plain— referred to as "Congaree Swamp"— along the Congaree River southeast of Columbia, S.C. The flood plain has an elevation slope and fall of 6 m from the upstream to downstream boundary. Hydrology is considered the most influential force driving landscape geomorphology and the forest dynamics of bottomland hardwood swamps indicative of a diverse and complex pattern of vegetative communities (Wharton and others, 1982; Thompson, 1998).

Forests of baldcypress (*Taxodium distichum*) and tupelo (*Nyssa* spp.) occupy low-elevation and flooded backswamp areas of old meander bends, while the higher flood plain zones are intermittently flooded and dominated by a diverse bottomland hardwood ecosystem interspersed with loblolly pine (*Pinus taeda*) populations. The operation of the Saluda Dam, 78 km upstream of the park, has reduced the magnitude, frequency, and duration of high flood events since its construction in 1930 (Whetstone, 1982; Patterson and others, 1985). Dam operation and streamside developments that could potentially change river stage and water quality, thereby posing a threat to forest diversity and productivity of Congaree Swamp, are major concerns of park management. Dewatering measures and flow regulation of river systems have led to water declines elsewhere that have propagated legal disputes among States and municipalities and put downstream ecosystems at risk.

Coastal Plain Forest Ecosystems

Congaree National Park represents a remnant old-growth forest under wilderness protection that is typical of Coastal Plain alluvial flood plain forest. Forests of the Coastal Plain region of the Southeastern United States are among the most productive in North America and form the basis of a large timber and wood products industry (Quarterman and Keever, 1962). Unmanaged forests in parks and preserves are an important complement to managed forests for critical wildlife and conservation needs (for example, Marks and Harcombe, 1981; Bridges and Orzell, 1989; Ware and others, 1993). Unfortunately, little quantitative data are available to facilitate the understanding of interannual variability and seasonality of climate and riverflow on Coastal Plain forest habitats. Few studies or tools are available to predict how Coastal Plain forest ecosystems will respond to either natural or anthropogenic changes in regional climate and watershed dynamics.

Old-growth forests are rare entities worldwide in need of special management and conservation measures. The Congaree National Park is a complex mosaic of wetland and upland forest associations that has been shaped largely by alluvial processes and natural climatic phenomena apart from any substantial influence by humans. The Congaree Swamp forests are among the tallest temperate deciduous forests, ranging from 30 to 50 m in height. Many State and national champion trees have been discovered at the park (Gaddy, 1977; Jones, 1997). Timber company records of parcels within the park indicated that baldcypress was selectively logged around the turn of the 20th century. Otherwise, half of the park area (4,450 ha; R. Sharitz, University of Georgia, Savannah River Ecology Laboratory, oral commun.) is regarded as old-growth forest that has escaped intensive or extensive land-use activities by humans except primitive access roads for hunting purposes.

Productivity Studies of Coastal Plain Forests

Long-term forest observations are valued commodities for determining the sensitivity and response of biological systems to environmental change. The ability to distinguish long-term changes in forests from short-term fluctuations caused by riverflow alterations or climatic anomalies may be impossible without long-term monitoring and tree-ring studies. For example, results of a long-term study at Big Thicket National Preserve demonstrated that only now, after 20 years of continuous observations, can long-term trends related to human activities be distinguished from short-term responses to natural climatic perturbations (Harcombe and others, 1998). Generally, abrupt changes in the flood regime of a swamp environment, drier or wetter, can lead to abrupt change in growth response of flood-tolerant bottomland hardwood species (Conner and Day, 1992; Keeland, 1994; Young and others, 1995). Studies of baldcypress growth have shown that flowing and fluctuating water regimes stimulate more growth and healthier trees than do stagnant and continuously flooded swamps (Brown, 1981; Lugo and Brown, 1984; Conner and Flynn, 1989; Dicke and Toliver, 1990; Megonigal and Day, 1992). Changes in water quality such as increased nutrient concentrations can spur increased forest productivity in receiving wetlands (Hesse and others, 1998; Day and others, 2006). Dewatering effects leading to streamflow reduction in the Apalachicola River flood plain ecosystem over the last few decades were shown to shift forest composition toward drier forest types of fewer flood-tolerant tree species (Darst and Light, 2008). In Congaree Swamp, forest plots were established to inventory the damage and recovery of bottomland hardwood forests following Hurricane Hugo in 1989 (Putz and Sharitz, 1991; Sharitz and others, 1993; Allen and others, 1997; Allen and Sharitz, 1999); these plots have been remeasured every 4 years since and may offer some much needed insight into the rate and process of forest regrowth and regeneration as related to disturbance and flood history.

Tree-ring studies of temperate forest species offer the means to quantify forest productivity, to examine climate-growth relations, and to relate growth patterns to environmental effects and disturbance events (Fritts, 1976; Fritts and Swetnam, 1989). Tree rings from old-growth sites provide centuries of climate information on the basis of ring size and density as opposed to relatively short-term observations from the existing network of meteorological stations within the Coastal Plain region, most of which were placed in service post-1948. Streamflow and drought reconstructions from tree rings of baldcypress have been achieved to determine the probabilities of water surplus and deficit cycles in select watersheds in Arkansas and North Carolina over millennial time scales (Stahle and others, 1985, 1988; Cleaveland, 2000). Baldcypress forests in coastal river outlets of South Carolina demonstrated negative growth effects from salinity exposure elevated by extended droughts, high sea level, and storm surge overwash from tropical storms (Doyle and others, 2007). Tree growth variations in flood plain sites dominated by baldcypress along the Savannah River below Thurmond Lake Dam, Ga., demonstrated growth alterations synchronously affected by streamflow regulation with dam operation (Palta, 2005). Cook and others (2001) conducted a regional assessment of climate history for the West Gulf Coastal Plain including parts of Louisiana and east Texas by using tree-ring chronologies from 38 site locations within and surrounding Big Thicket National Preserve. Their analysis chronicled the effects of logging and settlement periods, prolonged drought episodes, and hurricane disturbance in the region. Differences in the sensitivity of species to seasonal rainfall, drought, and temperature extremes were identified between pine and prominent hardwood species. The density of record-size trees in Congaree Swamp provided a comparative opportunity to further our understanding of how climate and flooding interact to control productivity and species response in South Atlantic Coastal Plain ecosystems.

Environmental Setting

Congaree Swamp

Congaree National Park is a unit of the National Park Service located in the South Carolina Midlands, approximately 35 km southeast of the State capital, Columbia (fig. 1). The park was established as a national monument in 1976 when Congress set aside 6,126 ha to protect an outstanding example of an old growth bottomland hardwood forest, known as Congaree Swamp. Considered the largest remaining intact tract of its kind in the United States, this unique wetland ecosystem was preserved for scientific, educational, and recreational purposes. In 1988, Congress funded the expansion of the park boundaries by designating 6,075 ha as wilderness and 2,768 ha as potential wilderness, bringing the total acreage

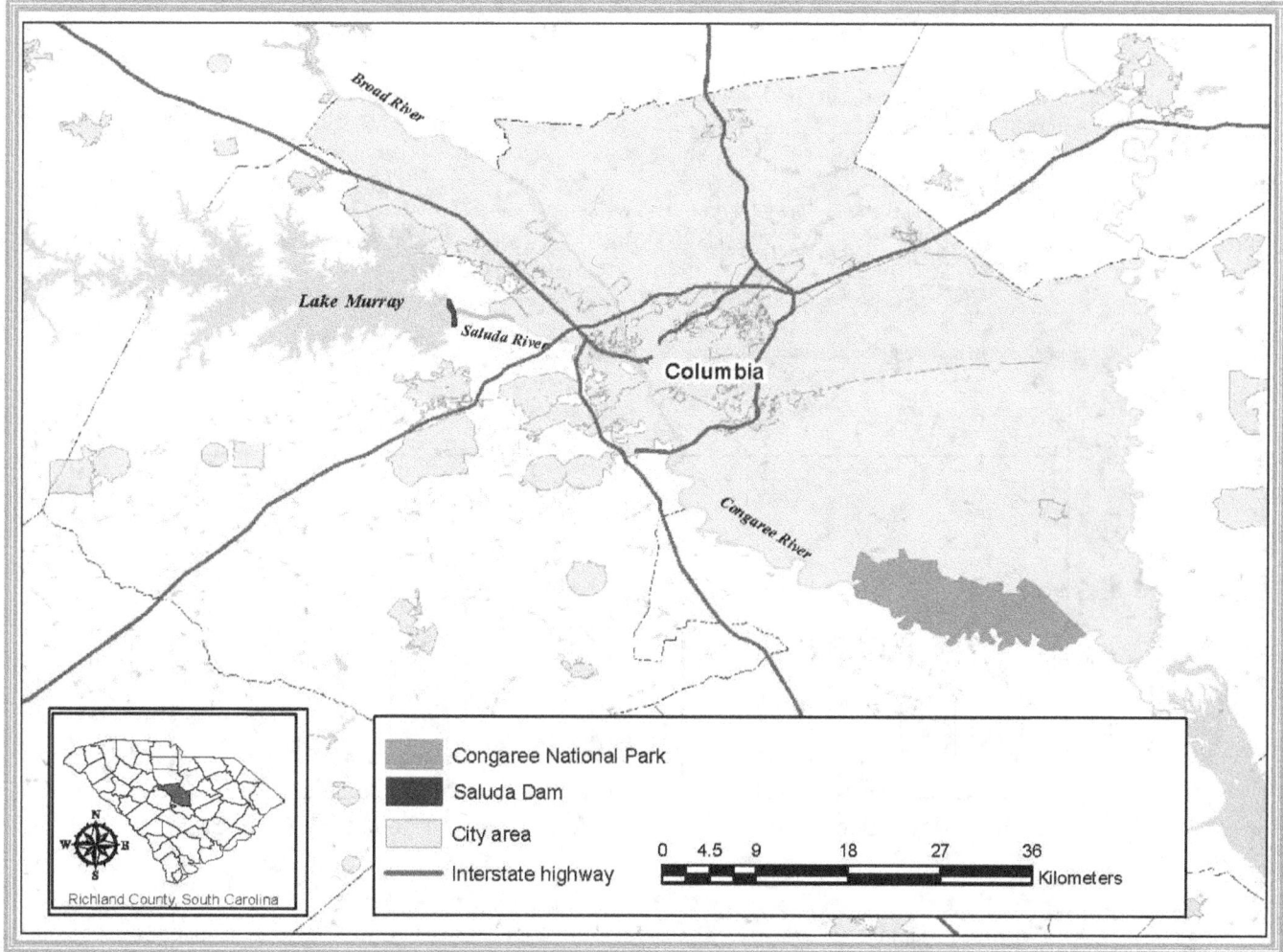

Figure 1.   Map of the South Carolina Midlands showing the public lands, rivers, lakes, and location of Congaree National Park, approximately 35 km southeast of the State capital, Columbia.

of the park to approximately 8,900 ha. In 2003, the South Carolina congressional delegation introduced legislation to elevate the status of the park from its early beginnings as a monument to that of a national park. In addition, the legislation expanded the park's eastern boundary by 1,862 ha, stretching southeast to the confluence of the Congaree and Wateree Rivers.

Congaree Swamp is situated in the southeast corner of Richland County along the north bank of the Congaree River. The lands surrounding the swamp are mostly cultivated for agriculture and timber production, but commercial and industrial interests are encroaching from upstream. The Congaree Swamp floods on average 10 times a year from flashy, short-duration pulses (Patterson and others, 1985). The Congaree River originates with the confluence of the Saluda and Broad Rivers in the City of Columbia.

Saluda Dam

Saluda Dam was completed in the early 1930s to create Lake Murray, a large hydroelectric reservoir, from the Saluda River near its confluence of the Broad River and headwaters of the Congaree River. Construction was initiated on September 21, 1927, and was completed on June 30, 1930. The drainage area of the Congaree River basin is approximately 21,471 km². A real-time gage is maintained by the U.S. Geological Survey (USGS) on the left bank at the southwest boundary of the park at river mile 150.7 (lat 33°48'38'', long 80°52'02'', Richland County, S.C.).

Climate

The entire park boundary and all sampling sites are located within Richland County, S.C., and Division 6 of the National Oceanic and Atmospheric Administration (NOAA) State Climate Divisions for South Carolina. Monthly climate data were obtained for air temperature, precipitation, and Palmer Drought Severity Index for the period of record from 1895 to present from the NOAA National Climatic Data Center.

Temperature

Mean monthly temperature ranges from a winter low in January of 7.7°C to a summer high in July of 26.9°C (fig. 2A). The mean spring/summer temperature pattern from March to August during the growing season for trees varies from year to year from lows near 20.5°C to highs near 23.1°C (fig. 2B). A 7-year running mean of spring/summer temperature exhibits abrupt swings in high versus low periods (fig. 2C). A general trend can be detected showing monotonically increasing temperature over the first 55 years from 1900 to 1955 followed by a rather sharp decline in temperature to a centennial low beginning in the early 1960s followed by an incremental rise to the end of the 20th century (fig. 2C). This spring/summer trend in the long-term temperature pattern closely follows the number of months of above average monthly temperature for the entire year, indicating dramatically hotter and cooler years for single and successive years (fig. 2D).

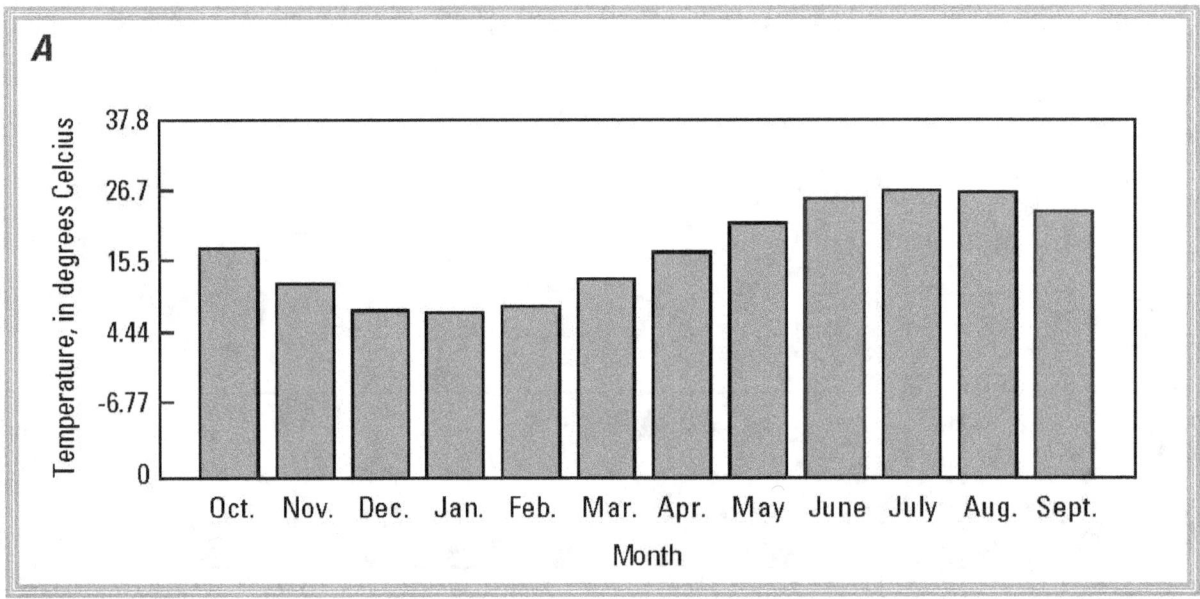

Figure 2.   Temperature records for the central region (Division 6) of South Carolina by month and year for the period of record from 1895 to 2007 (data source: National Oceanic and Atmospheric Administration, National Climatic Data Center, Asheville, N.C.). *A,* Mean monthly temperature by year for the period of record. *B,* Mean spring/summer (March–August) temperature by year. *C,* A 7-year running mean of spring/summer temperature. *D,* Number of months with above average monthly temperature by year.

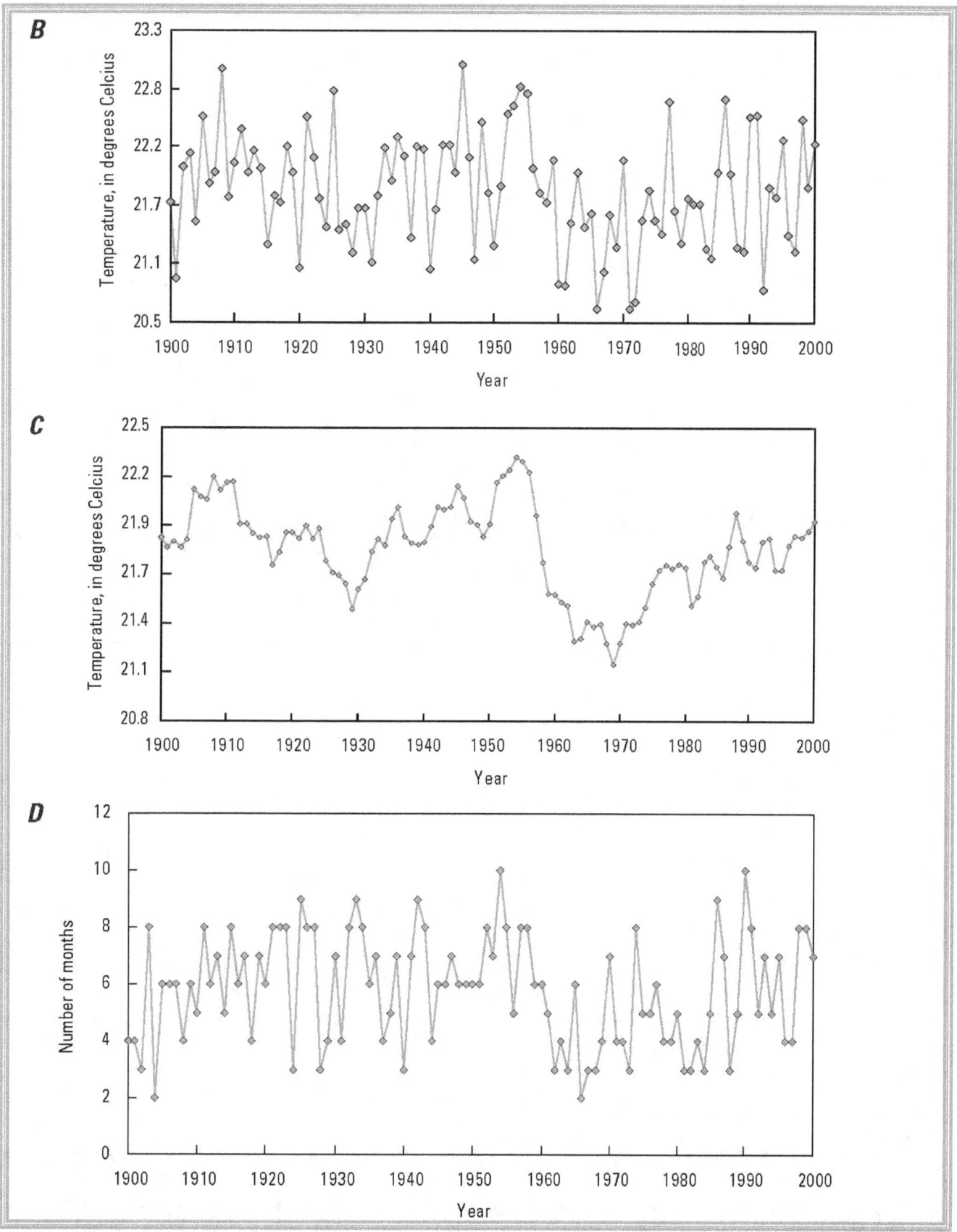

Precipitation

Mean monthly precipitation ranges from a winter low in November of 6.0 cm to a summer high in July of 13.8 cm (fig. 3A). The spring/summer precipitation pattern from March to August during the growing season for trees varies from year to year from lows less than 6.4 cm per month to a high near 17.8 cm per month (fig. 3B). A 7-year running mean of spring/summer precipitation exhibits a zig-zag pattern of high and low periods (fig. 3C). The number of months with above average precipitation shows a fairly evenly distributed pattern of wet and dry years (fig. 3D).

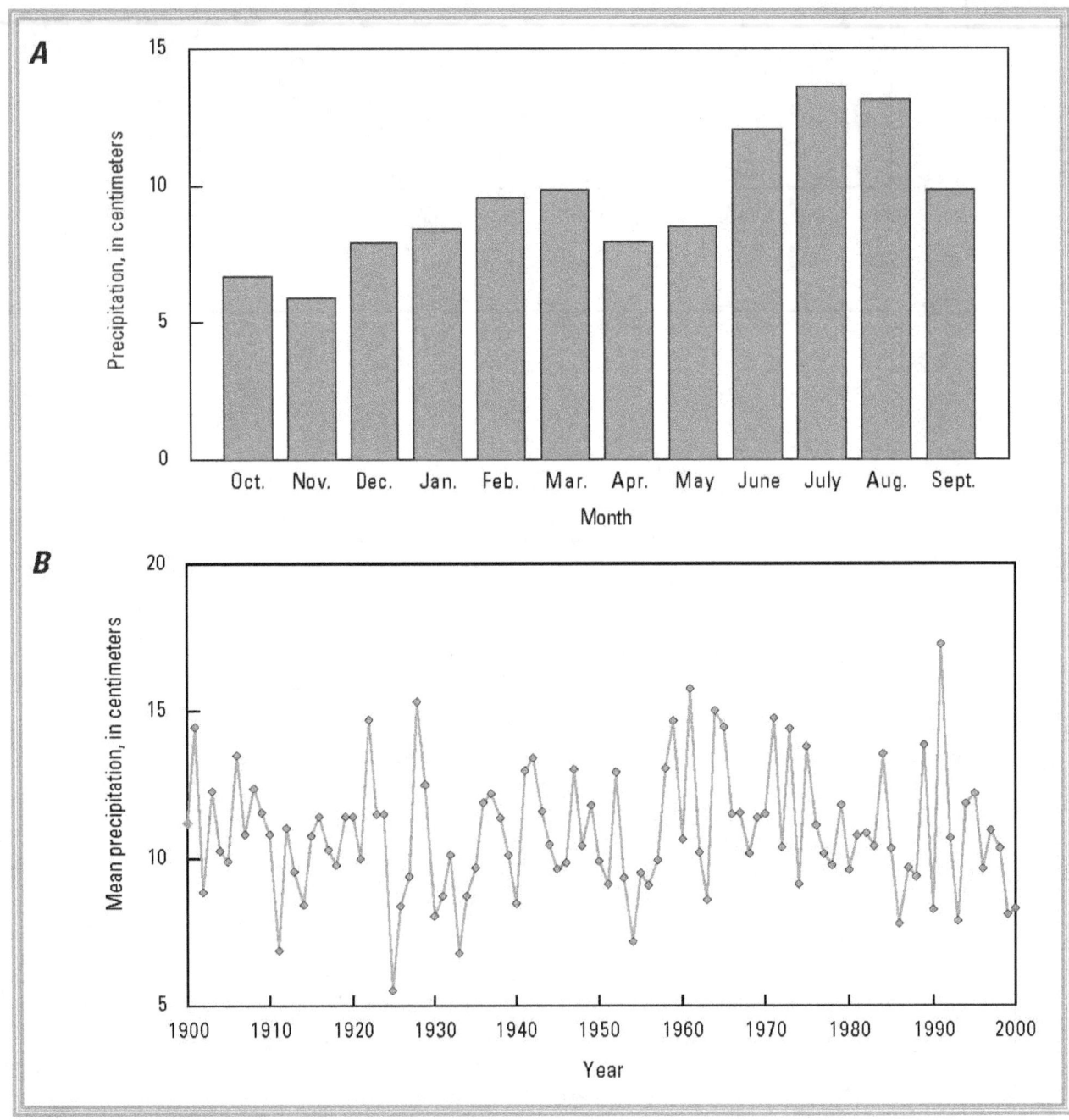

Figure 3. Precipitation records for the central region (Division 6) of South Carolina by month and year for the period of record from 1895 to 2007 (data source: National Oceanic and Atmospheric Administration, National Climatic Data Center, Asheville, N.C.). A, Mean precipitation by month for the period of record. B, Mean spring/summer (March–August) precipitation by year. C, A 7-year running mean of spring/summer precipitation. D, Number of months with above average monthly precipitation by year.

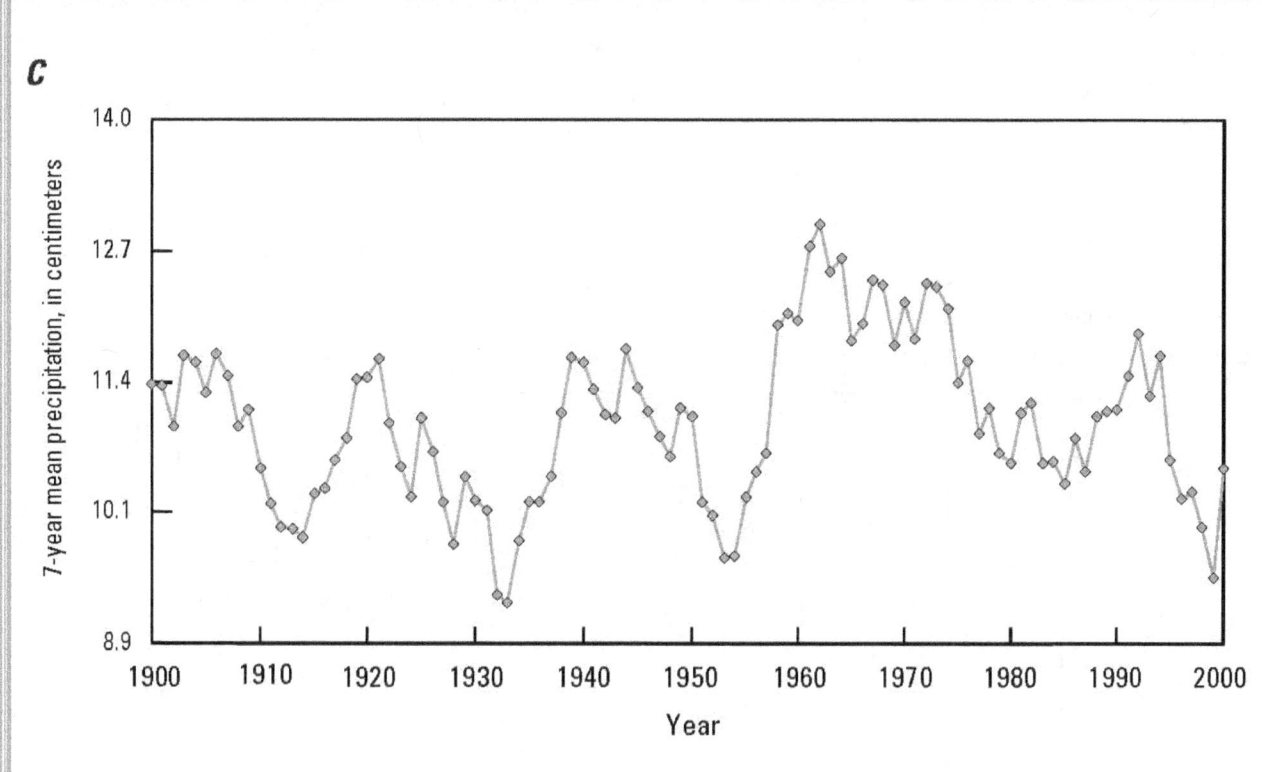

C

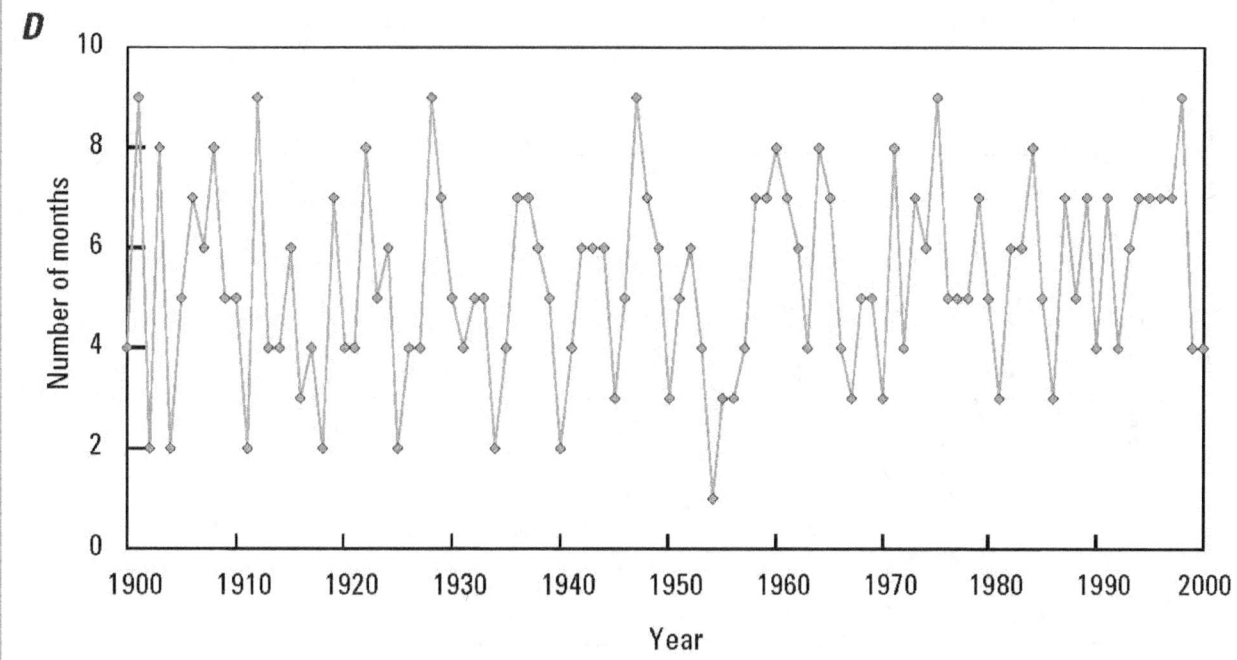

D

Palmer Drought Severity Index

The Palmer Drought Severity Index (PDSI) is an integrated function of precipitation and temperature that approximates soil moisture recharge predicated on current month conditions and previous month index values on a relative scale from +6 to -6 (positive values indicate wetness, and negative values indicate dryness and prevailing drought) (Palmer, 1965). Mean monthly PDSI ranges from a spring low (May) of -0.35 to a summer (June) high of -0.08 (fig. 4A). The spring/summer PDSI pattern fluctuates from +4 to -4 in the March–August growing season (fig. 4B). A 7-year running mean of spring/summer PDSI exhibits an oscillating downward trend to the mid-1950s before rising sharply to a high of +1.5 by the early 1960s followed by another downtrend to the mid-1980s followed by another upturn and downturn by the end of the century (fig. 4C). The number of months with above average PDSI by year exhibits a distinct multiyear drought period in the 1950s (fig. 4D). The seasonal and annual trends for PDSI generally follow the pattern of precipitation and to a lesser degree have an inverse relation with temperature.

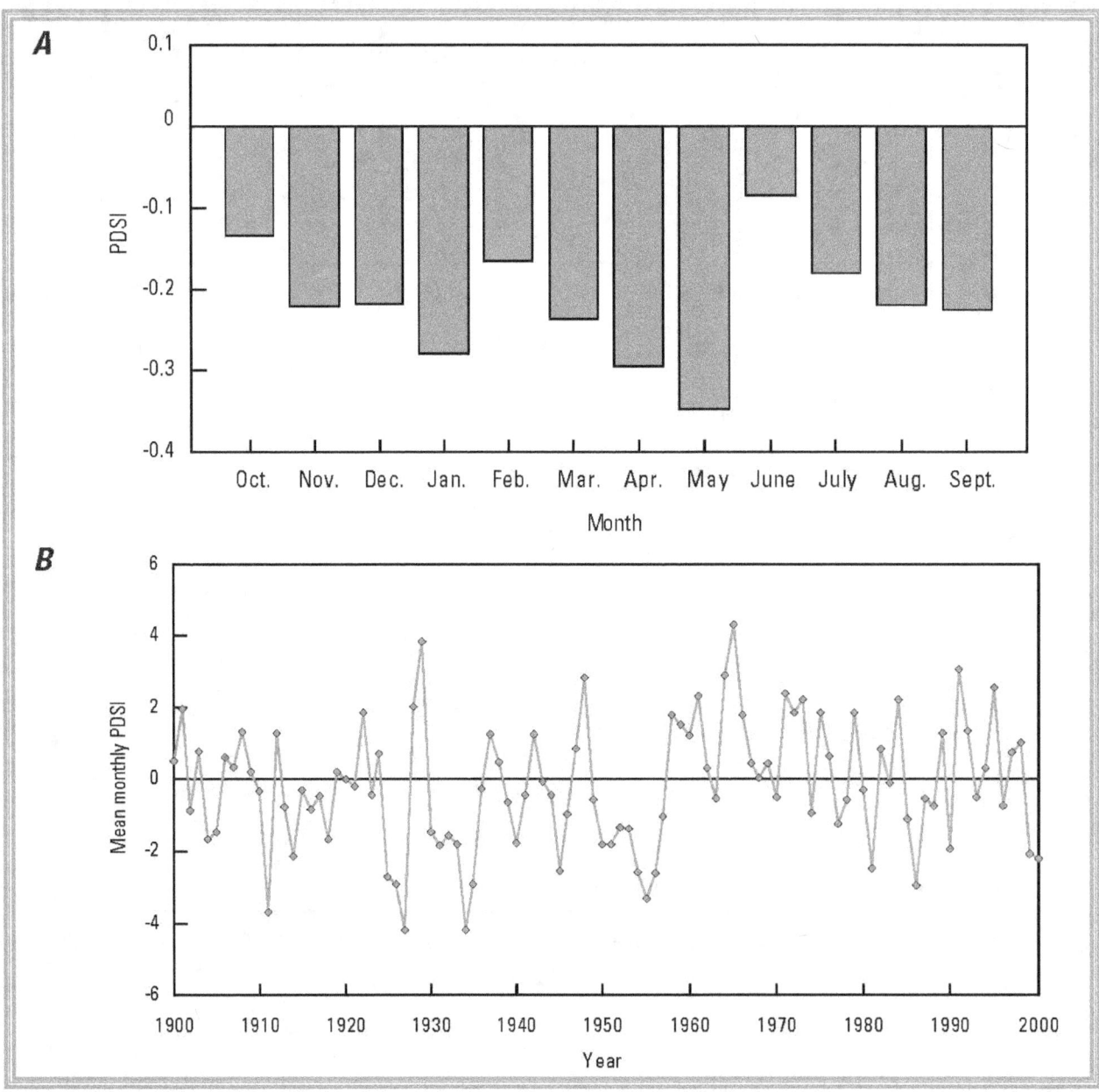

Figure 4. Palmer Drought Severity Index (PDSI) records for the central region (Division 6) of South Carolina by month and year for the period of record from 1895 to 2007 (data source: National Oceanic and Atmospheric Administration, National Climatic Data Center, Asheville, N.C.). A, Mean PDSI by month for the period of record. B, Mean spring/summer (March–August) PDSI by year. C, A 7-year running mean of spring/summer PDSI. D, Number of months with above average monthly PDSI by year.

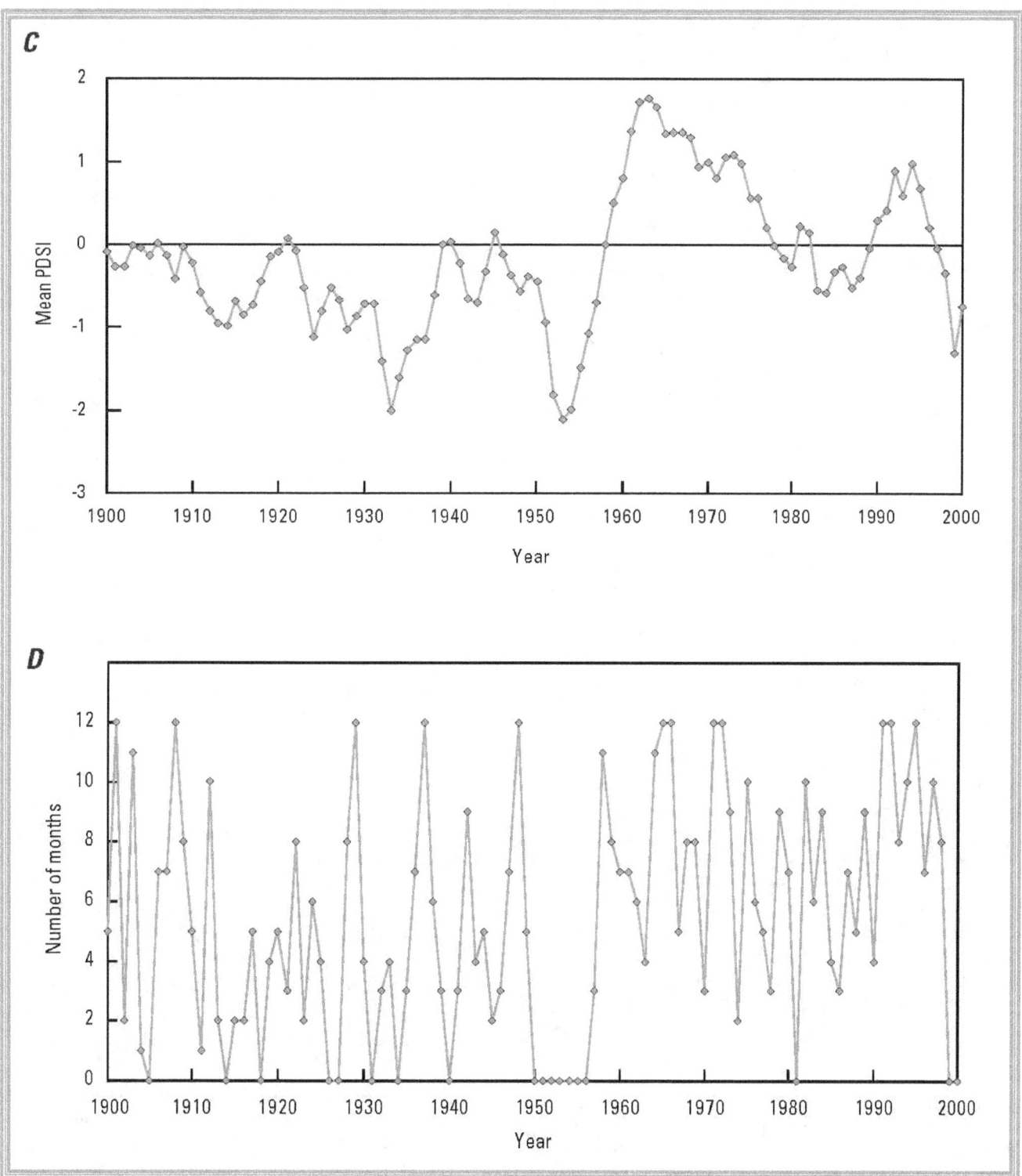

Hurricanes

Hurricanes are large-scale climatic phenomena that generate high winds, tidal surges, and inland floods responsible for wide-area damage and destruction of developed property and forest resources. Direct effects of windthrow, branch breaking, and leaf stripping are commonly observed within storm swaths that can be tens and even hundreds of miles wide and long as storms move inland. The disturbance impacts of major hurricanes on stand structure, composition, and successional processes on bottomland hardwood forests were investigated after Hurricane Hugo in 1989 (Gardner and others, 1991; Gresham and others, 1991; Hook and others, 1991; Putz and Sharitz, 1991) and Hurricane Andrew in 1992 (Doyle and others, 1995). Even though Congaree National Park is inland from the coast, the strength of Hurricane Hugo was still producing low Category 3 winds (51.4 m/s) sufficient to cause moderate to severe treefall damage within the park (Putz and Sharitz, 1991; Sharitz and others, 1993) and lingering impacts on forest recovery and woody vine density (Allen and Sharitz, 1999).

Hurricanes can modify the growth potential of trees either by creating canopy gaps or by direct injury of crown branches and leaf loss that can add a confounding influence to interpreting growth trends (Doyle and Gorham, 1996). Generally, hurricanes lose strength as they make landfall and proceed inland. A hurricane simulation model, HURASIM (Doyle and others, 1995; Doyle and Girod, 1997), was applied to reconstruct hurricane history and windfield distribution over Congaree National Park to gain a perspective of the dates and magnitude of storms capable of inflicting forest damage and influencing tree growth in Congaree Swamp. Model results showed that Hurricane Hugo was the strongest storm (in terms of windspeed) to impact the park in the last 120 years (fig. 5). A total of 15 storms have been recorded from 1886 to present with at least tropical storm wind strength (>17.4 m/s) passing over the park. Of these, six were strong enough to circulate hurricane force winds above 33.0 m/s. Only two storms have exceeded 44.7 m/s winds over the last century, including Hurricane Hugo, indicating that some forest thinning and disturbance from hurricanes may occur once every 50–60 years. Some tree species show greater resistance to wind damage, most notably baldcypress, which is prominent in the Congaree Swamp (Putz and Sharitz, 1991; Doyle and others, 1995).

Tropical depressions and storms are also capable of causing major flood events in Coastal Plain and Piedmont rivers including the Congaree River. Because of the relative infrequency of storms, there is too little effect on overall mean river stage during summer and fall months of hurricane season to be an important factor on tree growth. Maximum river stage records for 1935–2000 show the expected rise in spring streamflow and corresponding flood potential with periodic tropical storms and weather systems in late summer and fall (fig. 6).

Purpose and Scope

The purpose of this ecological study was to assess, characterize, and predict the effects of hydrological fluctuations of the Congaree River on park resources. Study tasks focused on tree-ring analysis and the development of a flood inundation model to predict the effects of flood events and flood history on forest resources and visitor safety. Park management lacked the scientific basis and understanding of how riverflow and stage of the Congaree River influenced backswamp flood relations, forest productivity, and inundation of hiking trails. While hydrological studies have been conducted to predict floodwave behavior between river reaches, there has been nominal monitoring of the actual flood plain to relate flood patterns and flows in backswamp areas. The upstream Saluda Dam was constructed in the 1930s, creating Lake Murray and effectively reducing historical flood frequency and magnitude downstream (Whetstone, 1982; Patterson and others, 1985). Park officials were interested in knowing whether dam operations and river flow over the past century had influenced the productivity of tree species within Congaree Swamp. Specific project objectives included (1) monitoring backswamp water levels and surveying the elevation of park trails; (2) simulating flood plain inundation in relation to Congaree River stage; and (3) developing tree-ring chronologies of select species from different hydrogeomorphic settings to determine effects of flooding related to historical streamflow regulation.

Methods

Water Level Monitoring

To determine flood plain inundation with river stage, water level recorders (gages) were installed in drainage guts along the river and feeder creeks and sloughs within the interior backswamp zones (fig. 7). Gages were deployed across the landscape gradient in the upper, middle, and lower reaches of Congaree Swamp proximal to trail locations and tree-coring sites (fig. 8). Gages consisted of transducer units (Infinity model 210) programmed to record continuous hourly readings. Gages were installed in the fall of 2001, but because of a severe and prolonged drought, there was no backswamp flooding until late fall of 2002. In contrast, 2003 was a high water year that brought several extreme floods that resulted in destruction of some gages and hiking trail bridges, which hampered backcountry access and tree core collections. Water level data were collected over a 4-year period from late 2002 through the winter/spring of 2006.

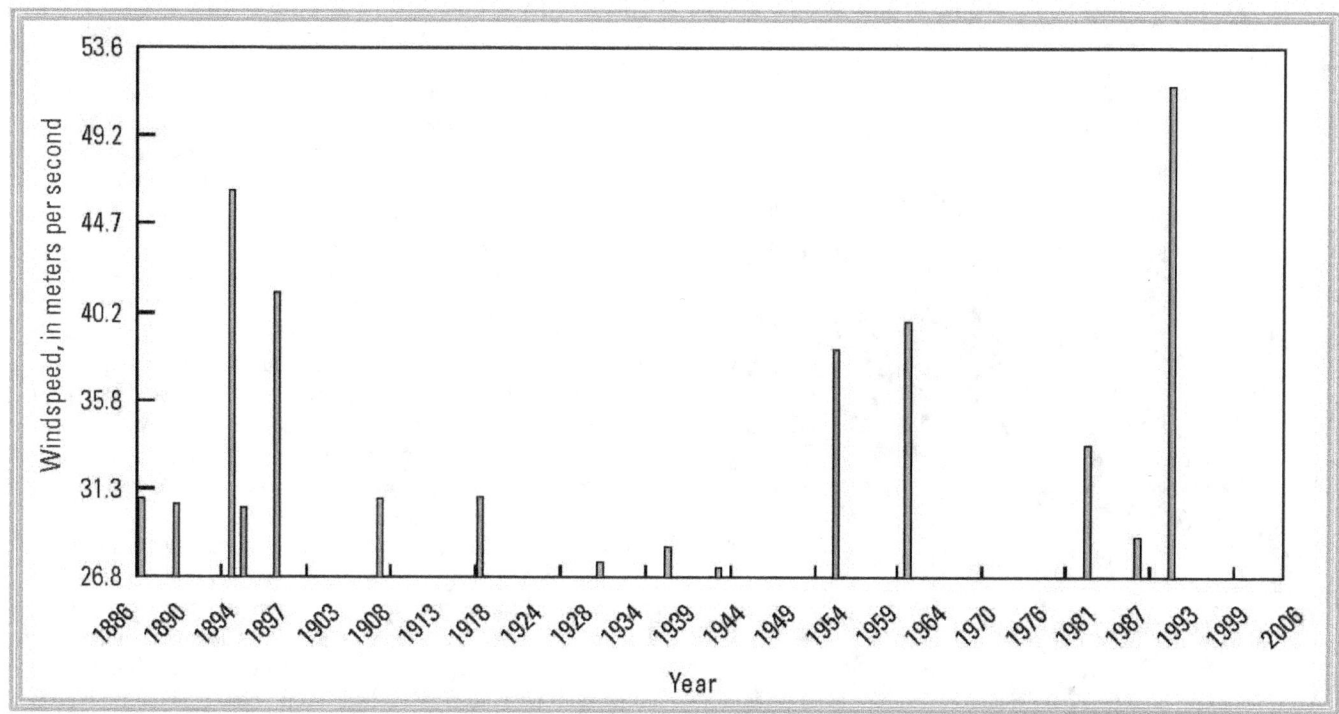

Figure 5. Chronology of estimated windspeeds at Congaree National Park from North Atlantic tropical storms and hurricanes passing over South Carolina in the last 120 years based on HURASIM model projections. A total of six storms of hurricane strength have impacted the park forests since 1886; Hurricane Hugo represents the strongest storm, with estimated windspeeds at 51.4 m/s.

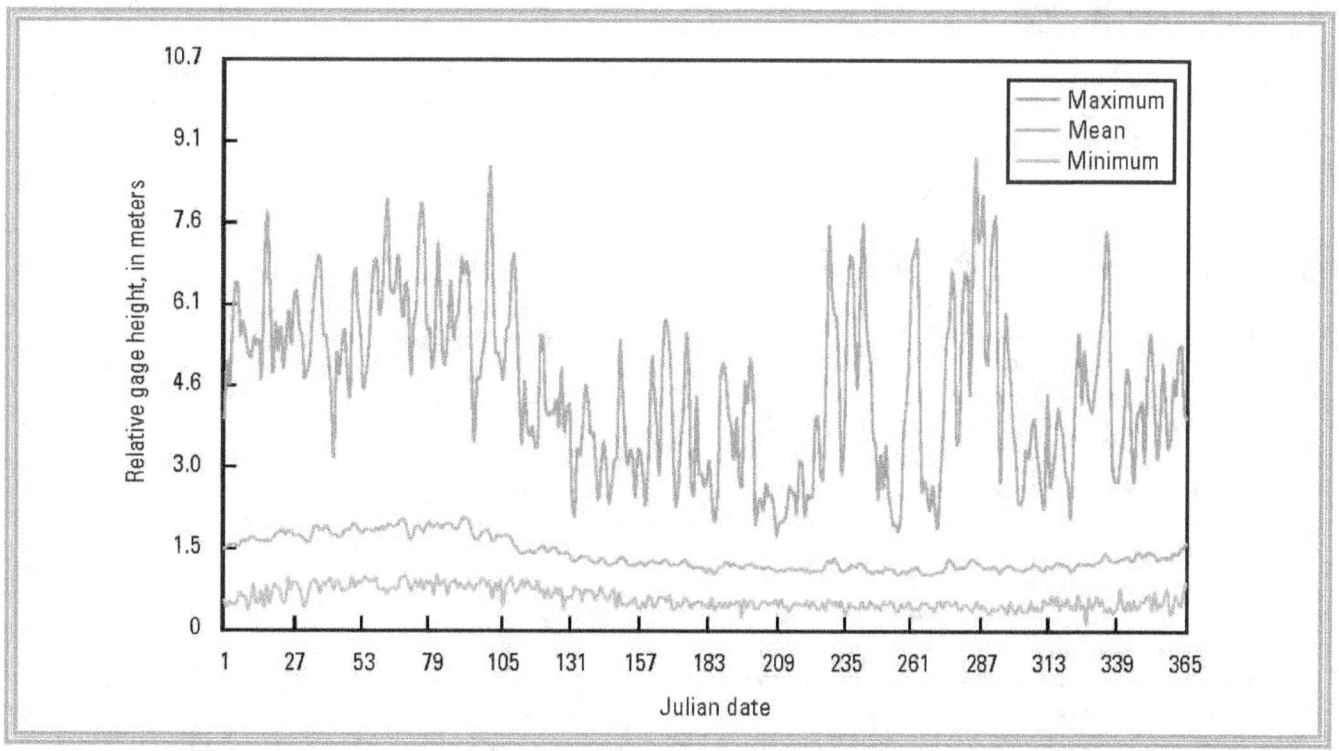

Figure 6. Average daily stage of maximum, mean, and minimum flows of the Congaree River at Columbia, S.C., by Julian date for the period 1935–2000, illustrating the expected rise in spring streamflow and corresponding flood heights with periodic tropical storms and weather systems in late summer and fall.

Figure 7. Photograph of water level gage (Infinity model 210) at Fort Motte railroad crossing on the lower Congaree River on the southeastern boundary of Congaree National Park.

Tree Core Collections and Measurement

Tree cores were collected from multiple species and forest stands to facilitate understanding of forest history and effects of flooding on long-term forest productivity. Species selection and sampling intensity focused on two primary conifer species and five secondary hardwood species to accomplish the development of tree-ring chronologies and age-size relations, respectively. Primary species selection included common conifer species, loblolly pine and baldcypress, on the basis of their wide distribution, various hydrogeomorphic settings, and contrasting flood tolerance. Multiple populations of each of these primary species were sampled across the flood plain in settings of greater or lesser flood retention and hydroperiod (temporary [dry], seasonal [bnk], and semipermanent [wet]; fig. 9). Some common hardwood species (green ash [*Fraxinus pennslyvanica*], laurel oak [*Quercus laurifolia*], swamp chestnut oak [*Quercus michauxii*], sycamore [*Plantanus occidentalis*], and water

tupelo [*Nyssa aquatica*]) were also cored to establish age-size relations and determine aspects of forest and flood history.

Three different types of hydrogeomorphic settings were identified within Congaree Swamp that were also associated with primary tree-coring sites described herein as riverbank, backswamp, and seepage zones. Riverbank areas are located directly adjacent to the main channel on the highest ground and on slopes defining the natural levee and full-bank stage. Trees in this zone usually include mixed hardwood species sometimes interspersed with baldcypress associates. Flooding is somewhat intermittent and seasonal, occurring during the highest flood events when reaching full-bank flood stage and usually of short duration in days or less. Backswamp areas are located beyond the natural levee in the interior flood plain at lower elevations that store floodwaters and remain inundated for longer periods. Seepage zones are old meander bends (oxbows) at the base of the flood plain escarpment that receive a fairly constant supply of groundwater seepage and surface water runoff from adjacent upland areas. These areas remain fairly saturated near soil surface year round but undergo deep flooding when the river stage nears full bank and overtops levees. Upland drainage and rainfall can also bring localized flooding in backswamp depressions and sloughs without river overflow.

Tree core and site collections were composed of 10–15 trees per species in proximity within a common hydrogeomorphic setting and forest stand. In all cases, two cores were extracted from opposite sides of each tree. Diameter at breast (core) height, tree height, and percent live crown were recorded for each tree to calculate stemwood production (basal area increment) from ring-width measurements and to associate crown class with tree vigor. In the case of buttswell trees and species, such as water tupelo and baldcypress in frequently flooded zones, cores were taken above the buttswell, usually 2–3 m above ground level. Standard dendroecological procedures were applied to collect, process, date, and measure annual growth rings (Stokes and Smiley, 1964). The dating process involved identifying a synchronous growth history within trees and sites and assigning a calendar year to each ring, the pattern of which corresponds with year-to-year variation associated with climate and environmental changes. Ring measurement was accomplished with the aid of a dissecting microscope, graduated stage, and optical encoder device to the nearest 0.01 mm. Ring measurements were checked for correct cross-dating with cross-correlation analysis.

Growth Calculations and Analysis

Radial measurements of growth rings of opposite radii and cores from each tree were used to calculate tree growth metrics, diameter increment, and basal area increment. Diameter increment (Dinc) is the increase in diameter for a particular year on a given tree. Annual Dinc is calculated by using the following equation:

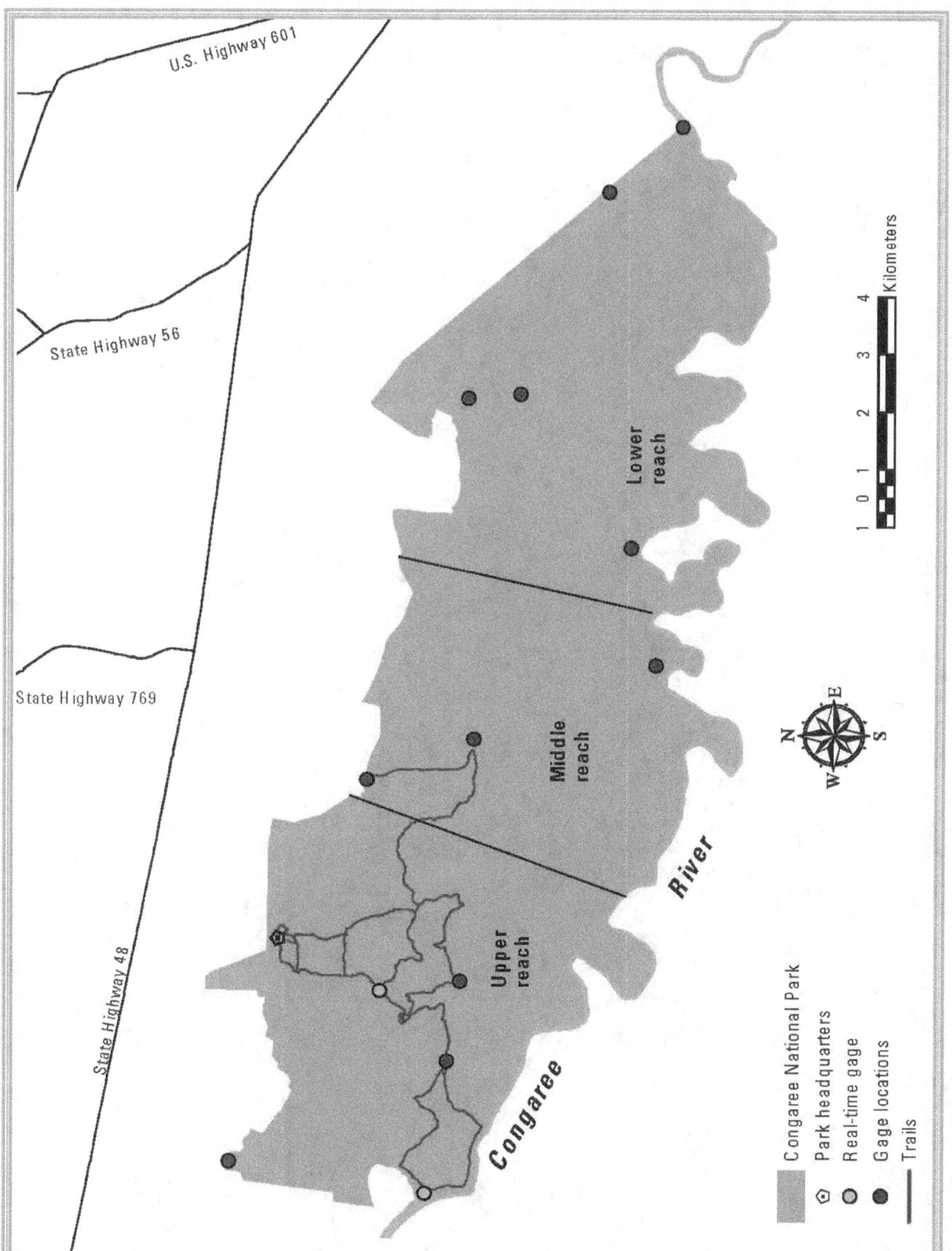

Figure 8. Map of water level gage locations within Congaree National Park in reference to longitudinal compartments that correspond to river grade (upper, middle, and lower river reaches).

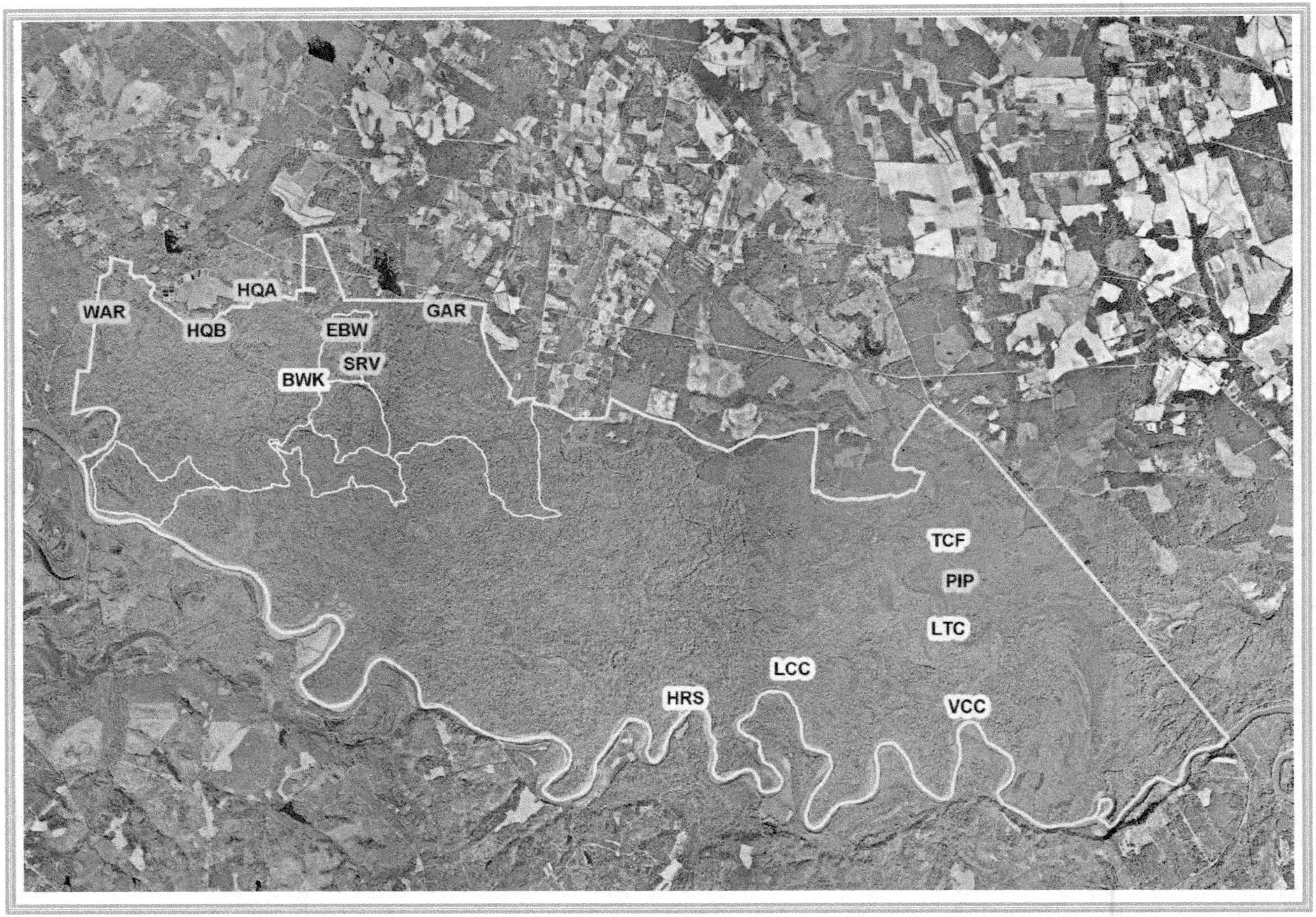

Figure 9.   Aerial photography mosaic of Congaree National Park showing locations of park boundary (light blue line), hiking trails (white lines), and tree-coring sites of primary species, baldcypress (yellow labels) and loblolly pine (green labels). Tree-coring sites for baldcypress included Boardwalk (BWK), Toms Creek flood plain (TCF), Lower Toms Creek (LTC), Horsepen (HRS), Lower Cedar Creek (LCC), and Virgin Cedar Creek (VCC). Tree-coring sites for loblolly pine included West Access Road (WAR), Headquarters A (HQA), Headquarters B (HQB), Elevated Boardwalk (EBW), Garrick Road (GAR), Service Road (SRV), and Pine Island Pines (PIP).

$$Dinc_t = rwA_t + rwB_t, \tag{1}$$

where $Dinc_t$ is the diameter increment of the tree in year (t), rwA_t is the measured ring width (rw) of core A for a given calendar year (t) on one radius of the tree, and rwB_t is the ring width of the same calendar year (t) of core B from the opposite radii of the same tree. Basal area increment (BAI) is the area of stemwood production for the entire growth ring for a given year for a tree of given size at year (t). Annual BAI is calculated by first decrementing diameter growth (Dinc) from measured diameter (Diam) at core height for every successive year and deriving the inside and outside radius of each ring boundary for the entire growth record:

$$BAI_t = ((Diam_t / 2)^2 * \pi) - (((Diam_t - Dinc_t) / 2)^2 * \pi) \tag{2}$$

BAI is the preferred and most comprehensive metric of tree growth given that it considers both the annual growth increment and size of tree. BAI is also more readily comparable between different chronologies and sites than is Dinc, which varies with tree age and size. Most trees and species will reach a stable BAI with canopy establishment for a given site quality and comparable canopy leaf area.

Tree-ring data constitute longitudinal data such that a subject class of individual trees (that is, site collection) is measured repeatedly on an annual basis (that is, ring widths). Single-year comparisons primarily identify climate-induced growth deviations of wet and dry year cycles, while multiyear growth comparisons isolate growth changes or inflections that may correlate with long-term climate trends or disturbance events, such as Hurricane Hugo or the Saluda Dam effect on riverflow changes. Growth response differences between age cohorts and different forest stands within a region are used to interpret the source of variation and disturbance type and magnitude. Normalized difference algorithms were used to compare within-tree variance related to stemwood distribution pattern that also chronicles the onset of stand-level disturbances, such as logging activities and hurricane disturbance (Doyle and Gorham, 1996). Mean chronologies were developed for primary tree species, baldcypress and loblolly pine, to relate long-term productivity with differences among sites that represent greater or lesser flood potential or hydroperiod. Sites of common hydrogeomorphic setting were grouped to allow analysis of flooding potential on growth performance and to evaluate species response to changes in hydrology before and after 1934 relating the effect of riverflow change from Saluda Dam construction and operation. A two-way analysis of variance (ANOVA) was used to test for differences between growth periods by species or hydrogeomorphic setting in the immediate periods prior to dam construction from 1915 to 1929 and the postdam period from 1935 to 1949.

Results

Hydrological and Trail Elevation Surveys

Long-term hydrological records exist for the Congaree River at Columbia dating from 1892 to present. Missing records in the data record were mostly caused by the impact of highest floods that damaged gage structure, mechanics,

or electronic components. Overall, the hydrological record for the Columbia gage is fairly robust with less than 5 percent of missing daily records (fig. 10*A*). Mean annual stage has increased slightly since 1940 in part by more evenly distributed flows released from the Saluda Dam for hydroelectric generation and likely changes in river gradient (fig. 10*B*). Water volume of floods on the Saluda River that passed downriver in hours and days prior to dam installation in the 1930s have since been stored in Lake Murray to be released days and weeks later, effectively raising the mean daily river stage of the Congaree River (Conrads and others, 2008). Maximum stage height shows the year-to-year extremes and variability of high and low flow years attributed to climate (fig. 10*C*). More years are near normal than extremely wet or dry by comparison. Typical high (1975) and low (1988) flow years are differentiated more by increased frequency of

singular flood events than by sustained water flow of higher or lower stage on a daily basis (fig. 10*D*).

These same data are useful for examining stage differences pre- and post-Saluda Dam operation to determine effects of discharge schedules and volume on downstream flow conditions and patterns. Counting the number of days that stage was equaled or exceeded for different stage heights provided some measure of river hydroperiod for comparison (fig. 11). While reports have been published to show that the Saluda Dam has effectively reduced the high flows and floodwaves of the Saluda River tributary (Whetstone, 1982; Patterson and others, 1985), stage relations showed that low and medium flows have actually increased following dam operation from more regulated discharge and flood storage capacity of Lake Murray (fig. 11). These data confirmed that, even though the dam was completed in 1930, several years

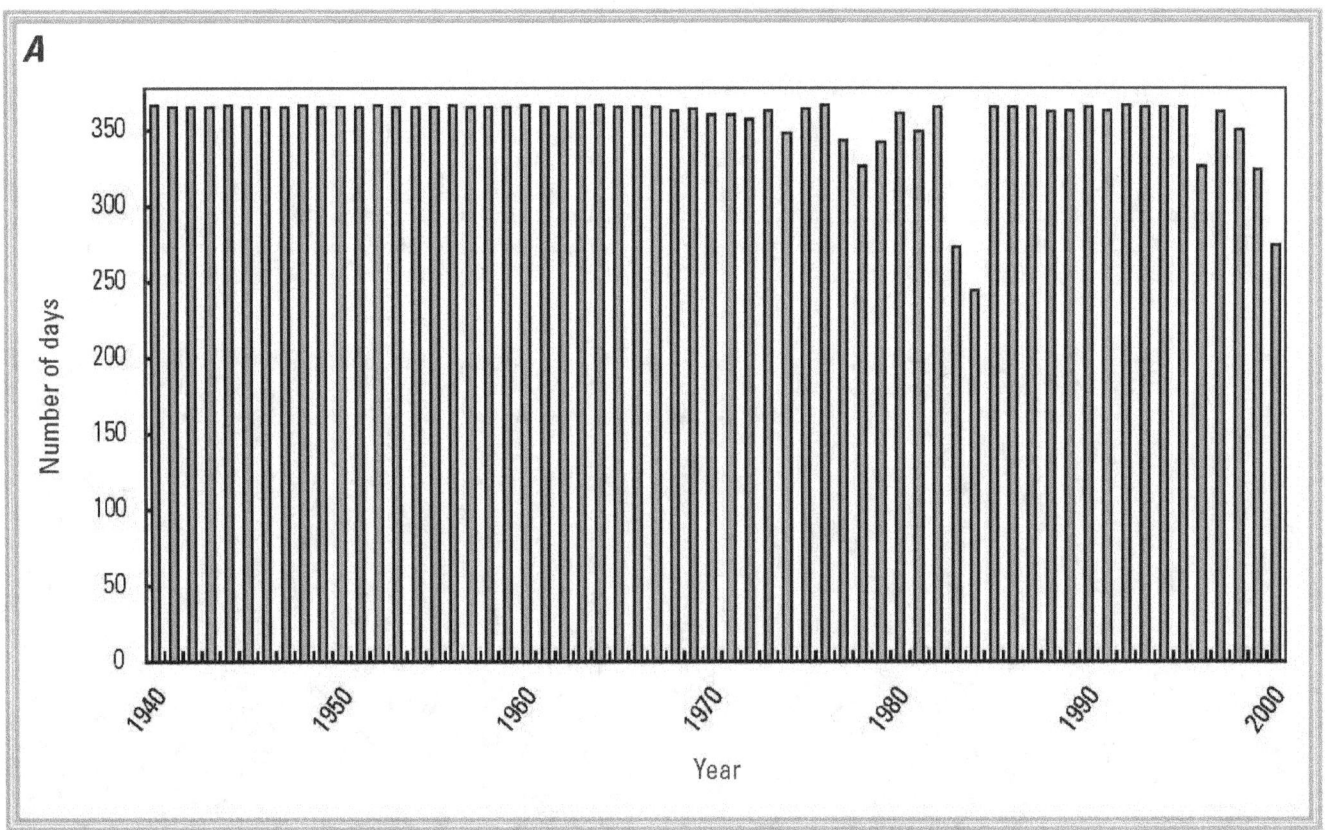

Figure 10.   Stage records for the Congaree River at Columbia, S.C. *A*, Number and pattern of missing daily records illustrating less than 5 percent of missing data from 1940 to 2000. *B*, Mean annual stage showing a slight rise since 1940 attributed in part by more evenly distributed flows released from the Saluda Dam for hydroelectric generation and likely changes in river gradient. *C*, Maximum stage height from 1940 to 2000 illustrating the year-to-year extremes and variability of high and low flows. *D*, Typical hydrographs from high (1975) and low (1988) flow years differentiated more by increased frequency of singular flood events than sustained water flow of higher or lower stage.

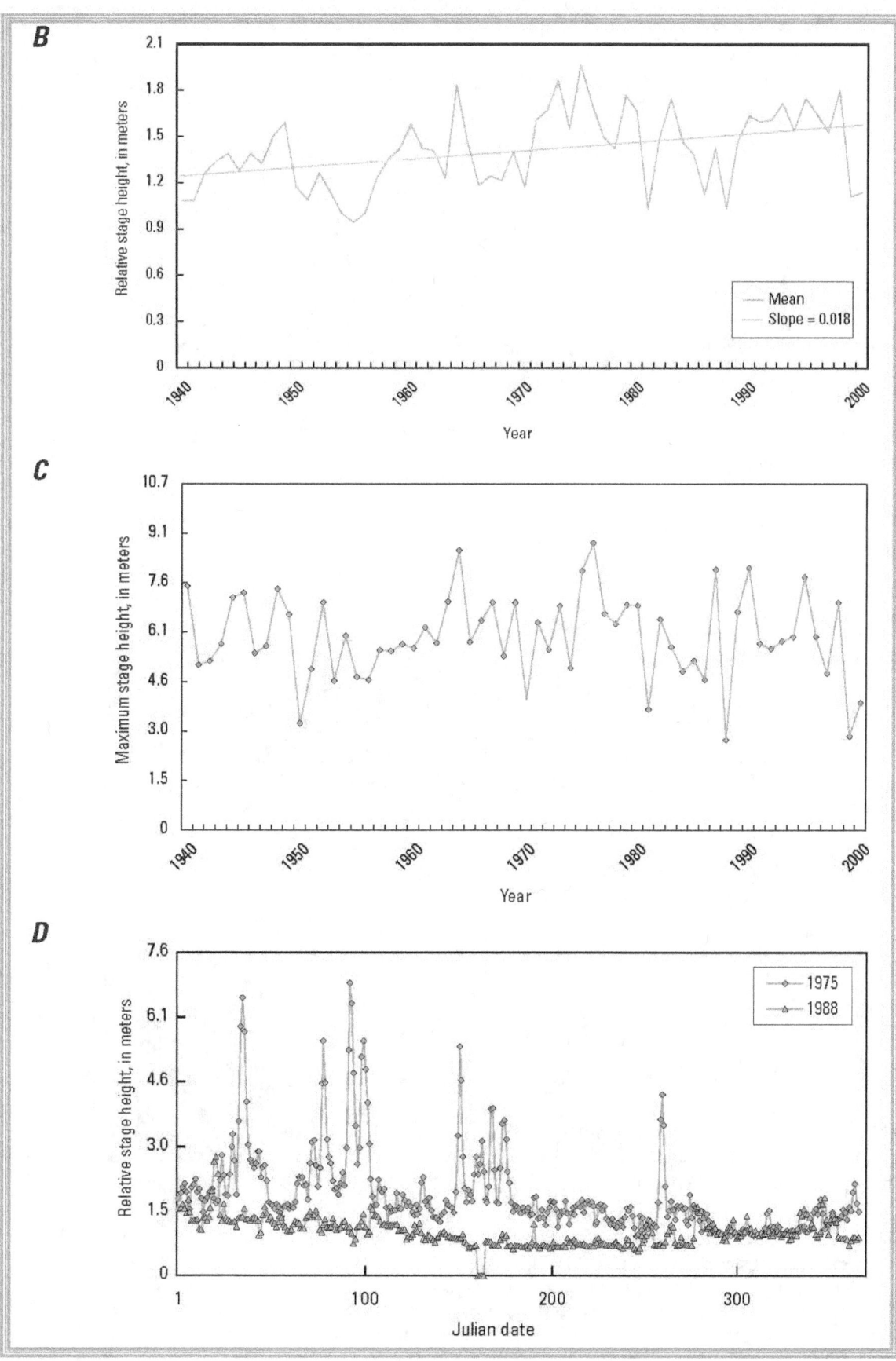

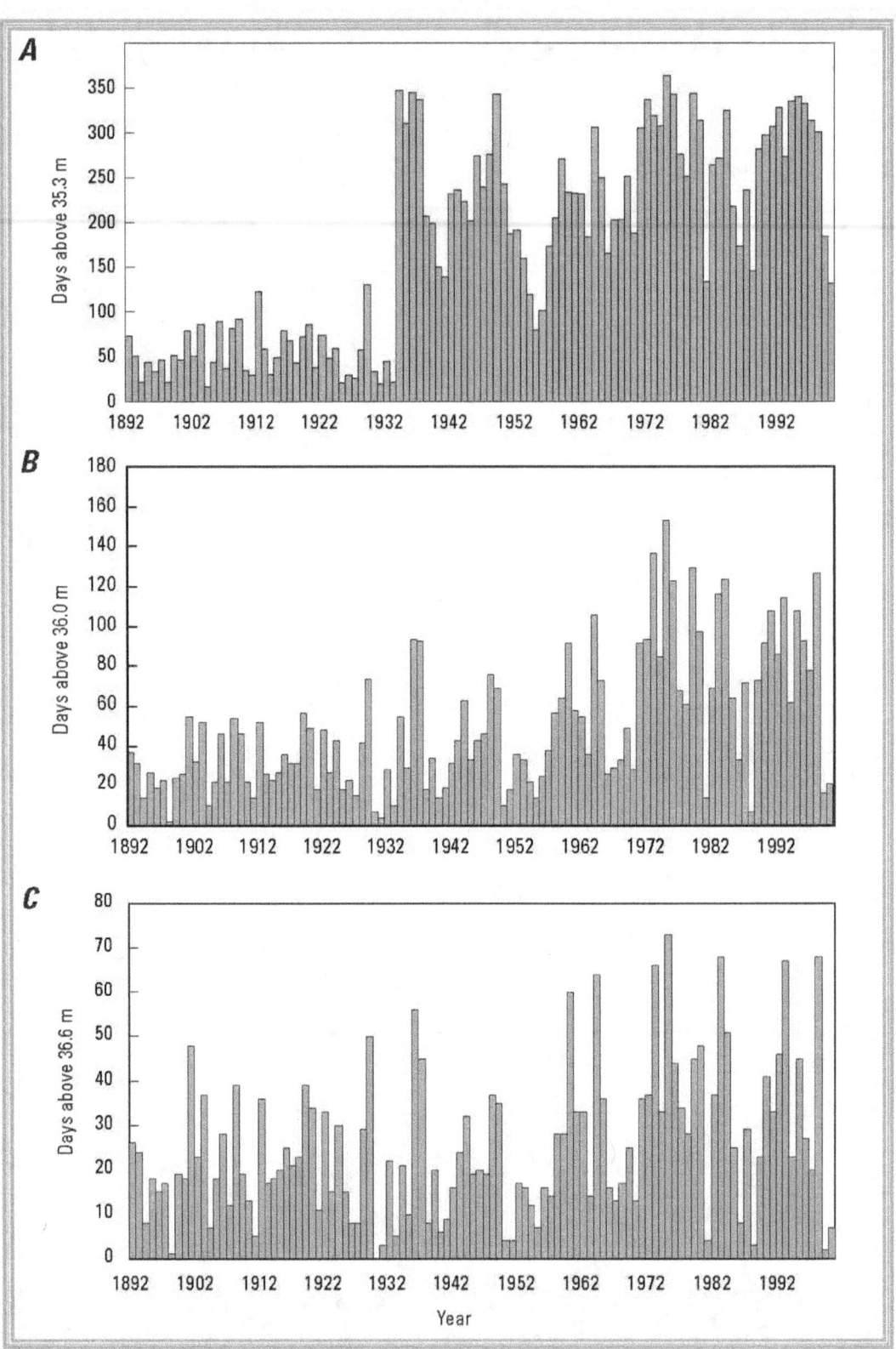

Figure 11. The number of days that water levels equaled or exceeded select stage heights for the Congaree River at Columbia, S.C., over the period of record from 1892 to 2000. Stage differences pre- and post-Saluda Dam operation circa 1934 illustrate an overall increase in low flows following dam installation. *A*, Stage height of 35.3 m. *B*, Stage height of 36.0 m. *C*, Stage height of 36.6 m.

were required to accumulate the streamflow and rainfall to reach permanent pool stage in Lake Murray by 1934. Analyses for testing flood effects on forest resources therefore utilized streamflow data preceding from before 1930 and after 1934 to represent predam and postdam streamflow conditions.

Water quality and flooding are major factors affecting wetland composition, structure, and productivity of flood plain ecosystems (Carter, 1986; Mitsch and Gosselink, 1993). The elevation of a given tract of forest or park trail and the degree to which the flood plain slope is coupled with the river stage determine the flood potential and local hydroperiod. Some systematic studies have been conducted in Congaree Swamp to describe the forest structure and composition in relation to land elevation and hydrologic forcing (Rikard, 1988); however, given the subtle local relief of this flood plain, greater vertical resolution was needed to model the flood contingencies of park trails and to calibrate a flood inundation model for predicting flood effects and forest response.

Park trails and water level gages within the Congaree River and flood plain were surveyed into a common datum to determine the degree of hydrological coupling with river stage. All park trails were explicitly surveyed with differential leveling by using laser level equipment and methods to establish surface elevations of soils and ponded water on a 10-m horizontal resolution and 1-mm vertical resolution (fig. 12). Elevation circuits inclusive of the entire trail system of the park met closure error and standards exceeding third-order vertical leveling criteria. The combined elevation circuits

inclusive of park trails were resolved into a digital elevation model. The digital elevation model of the trail system was then used in conjunction with hydrological surface models to create a flood plain inundation model for forecasting flood potential for current and next day conditions based on river stage at Columbia.

Flood Plain Inundation Model

A typical hydrograph of Congaree River stage and the Boggy Gut stage in the backswamp for the 4-year period (2002–5) demonstrated synchronous stage heights and coupling when river flows reached full bank and breached natural levee height (fig. 13). Some gages were damaged by extreme floods during 2003 and thereafter by fallen trees or debris flows and were not replaced. Spring and summer floods of 2003 also destroyed many trail boardwalks over sloughs and channels, which affected park access and visitation (fig. 14). Regression models were applied to establish autocorrelation in flood stage between gages at Columbia and those in the upper, middle, and lower reaches of the river and backswamp within the park. Flood relations between backswamp gages demonstrated greater flood retention and delayed recession behavior within the lower reach compared to the upper and middle reaches of Congaree Swamp.

A flood plain inundation model was developed for the park trail system on the basis of relations and regressions of

Figure 12. Photograph of trail at Congaree National Park and laser level equipment used to establish vertical elevations of ground and water surfaces.

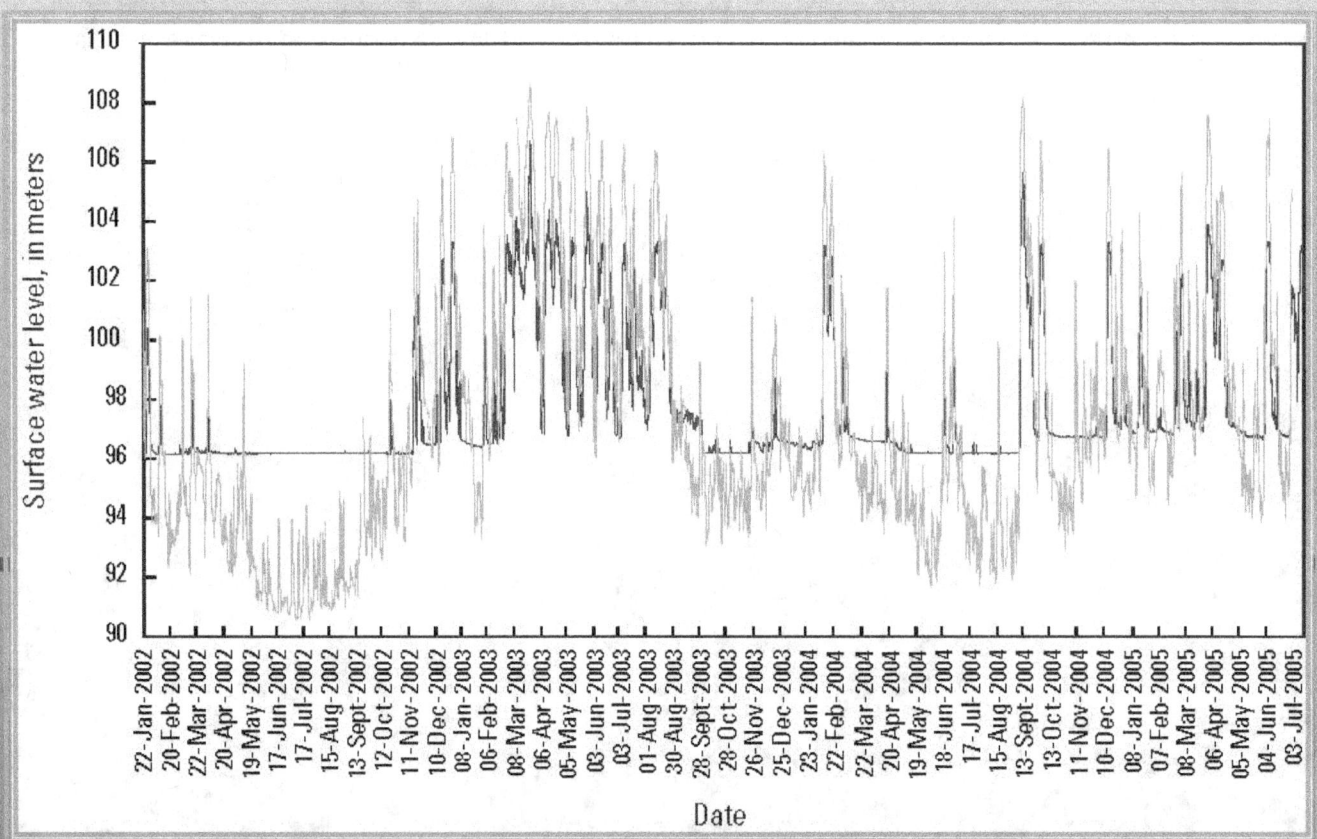

Figure 13. Typical hydrograph of Congaree River stage (gray line) and the Boggy Gut gage (red line) in the backswamp over a 4-year period (2002–5) showing synchronous stage heights and coupling when river flows reach full bank and breach natural levee height.

backswamp stage observations with Congaree River stage at the upper park boundary and its headwaters in downtown Columbia. Upstream and downstream gage relations were established between the Columbia gage and Congaree gage at the park boundary. Correlations of simultaneous records of stage heights showed flood loop relations of higher and lower stage heights relative to floodwave size, timing, and movement between gage locations (fig. 15A). The resultant data field is unsynchronized, showing a pattern of scattered points reflecting a range of gage relations below and above full-bank behavior. Time-step integration was used to account for a floodwave lag of 20 hours or more from Columbia to the upper park boundary that compresses the data field and more clearly shows gage coupling (fig. 15B). This envelope of stage relations allows a maximum and minimum flood relation of 0.3–0.6 m range for flood conditions below full bank and near 1:1 relations for overbank riverflow. The small variance of the flood envelope between gages is related to a number of factors, including antecedent conditions of rainfall and runoff contribution from uplands affected by recharge status and residual water storage within the Congaree Swamp and elsewhere upstream, and to the properties of the floodwave size and speed, which can vary depending on tributary contributions and timing of peak flows. The upper and lower cusps of the envelope defined the states where flooding effect is at a minimum and maximum, respectively (see fig. 15B). Local elevations below the lower cusp or maximum inundation

are always expected to be inundated, whereas elevations above the upper cusp are always above potential flooding and dry.

The same procedure was used for successive gages in the backswamp zone and downstream of the Congaree River gage involving lags of another 4 or more hours depending on distance downstream and from the river. Another example of the relation of the river gage at the Congaree gage and the Boggy Gut gage shows a best-fit of a 4-hour lag (fig. 16A). Dissecting the data into flood rises and falls shows how the river rises and falls first and the interior gut fills and drains at different stage relations (fig. 16B). Gage relations and functions were defined for all gage combinations and used to create a surface response model for each 3-cm increment of river stage at the Columbia gage.

The flood plain inundation model determines whether trail surfaces are dry or wet by contrasting the flood response surface heights for different river stage at the Columbia gage and the elevation of 1-m segments of the park trail digital elevation model (fig. 17). When trail elevations are above the predicted flood envelope, trails are dry. When trail elevations are below the flood envelope, they are inundated. When trail elevations are within the upper and lower flood envelope, they are considered wet and potentially flooded. The flood model was developed and tested to run on a Web-based server to allow park staff and beta testers to review model function and utility. By default the model uploads real-time and previous daily gage heights from the USGS National Water Information

Figure 14. Photograph of damaged trail bridge across a narrow drain in Congaree National Park following high floods in spring of 2003.

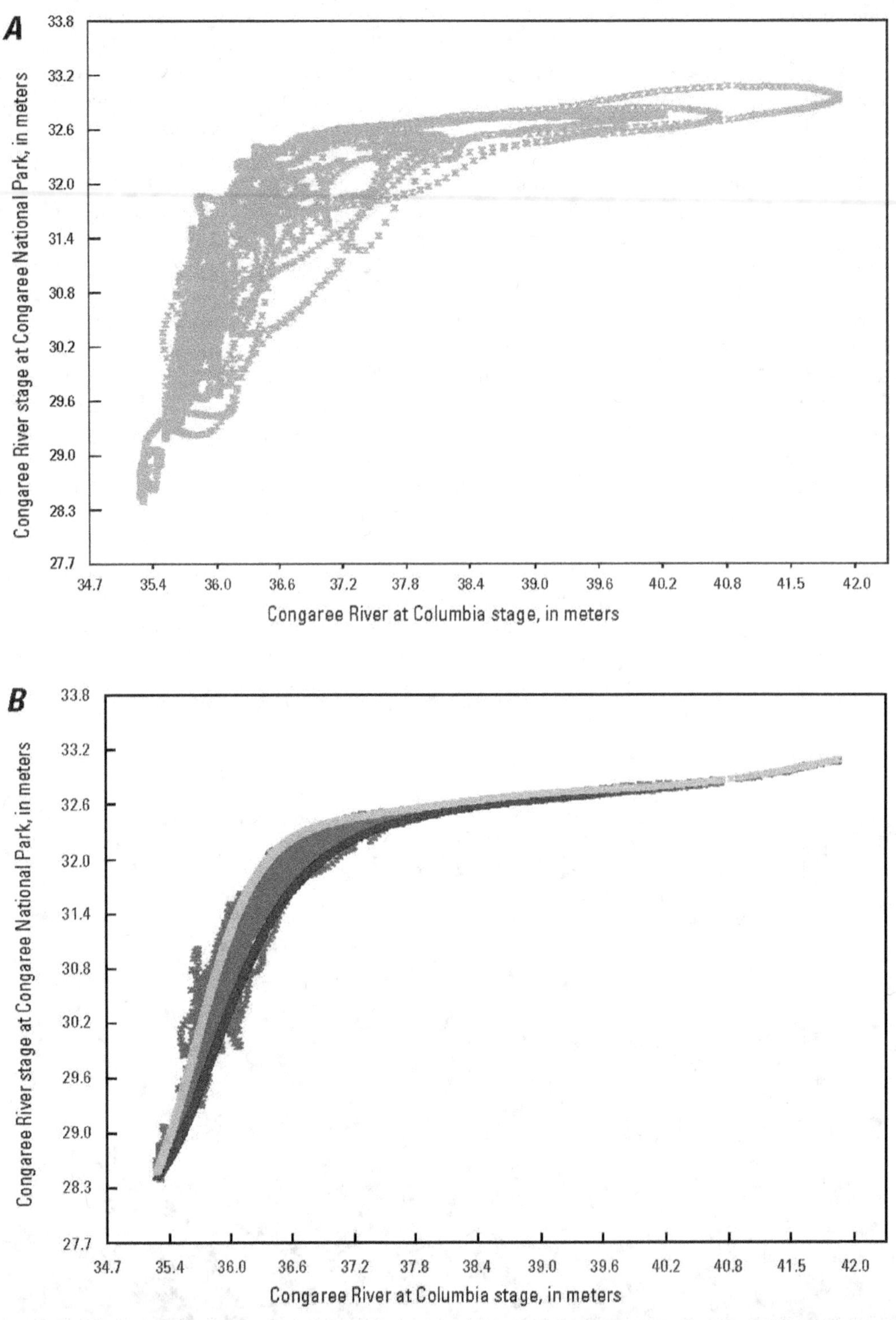

Figure 15.   Relation of stage height records and flood loop patterns for the upstream gage of the Congaree River at Columbia, S.C., and the downstream in-channel gage at the western boundary of Congaree National Park. *A*, Unshifted, simultaneous hourly readings. *B*, Shifted hourly readings of 20 hours to account for floodwave travel and coupling. The upper (tan line) and lower (red line) cusps of the envelope define the elevation where flooding is minimal and maximal, respectively.

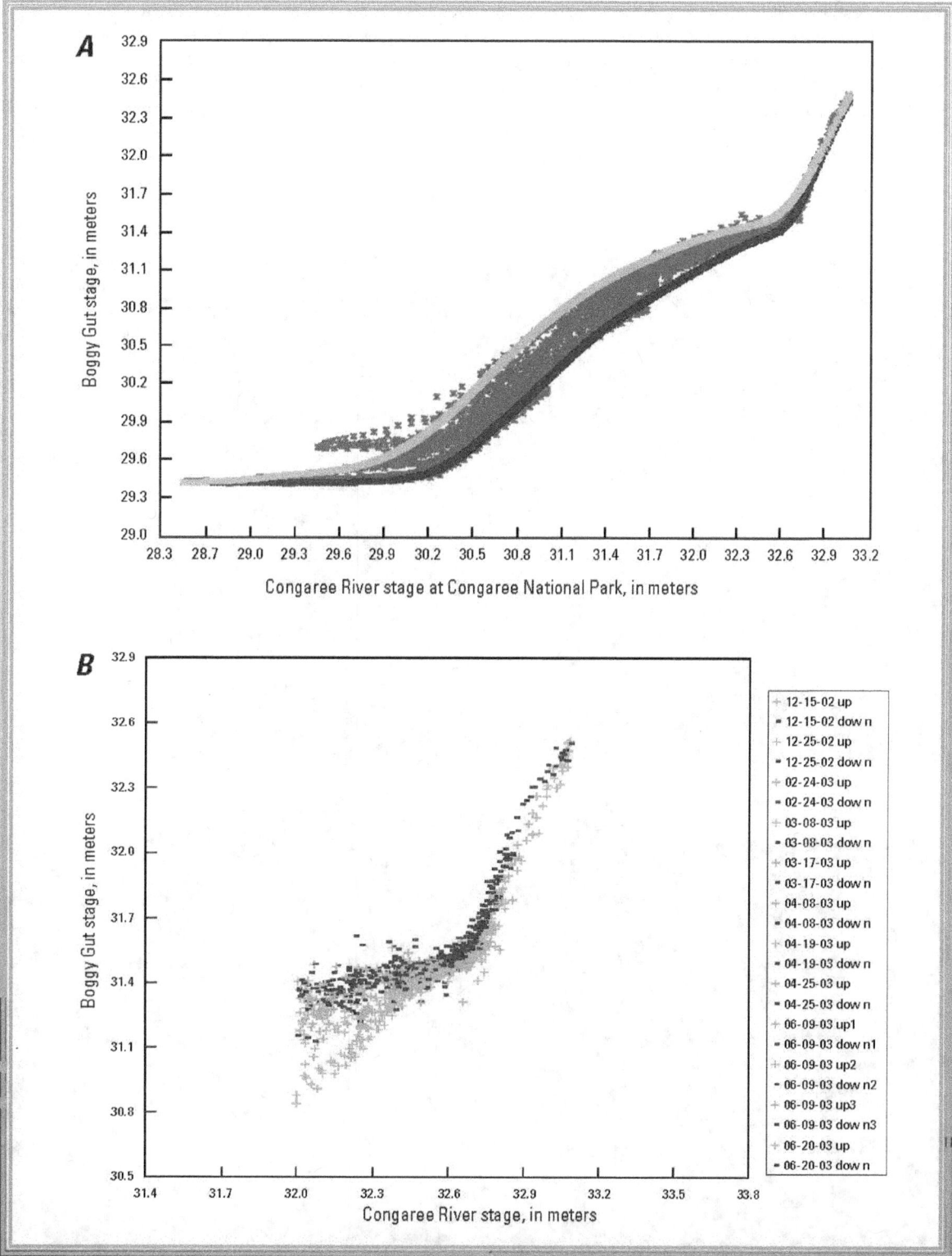

Figure 16. Stage relation of hourly readings from the Congaree River gage and the Boggy Gut gage in Congaree National Park. *A*, Shifted hourly readings with a best-fit 4-hour lag in floodwave travel. The upper (tan line) and lower (red line) cusps of the envelope define the states where flooding is minimal and maximal, respectively. *B*, Sorted hourly readings of flood rises (blue plus signs) and falls (red minus signs) illustrating the effect of timing and stage during the filling and draining of backswamp floodwater. Legend shows select flood events segregated by date and by rise (up) and fall (down) of passing flood wave.

System Web site to allow public access to online gage data and graphics at the Columbia gages and park gages on the Congaree River and Cedar Creek (fig. 18). This function allows users to check current river stages in the Congaree basin and allows the flood inundation model to forecast the 24-hour flood condition on the trail network within the park. Features were added to allow users to manually insert stage heights for the Columbia gage to see how the various trails undergo predicted inundation with higher river stages (fig. 19). Users can also select a specific trail system of interest to enlarge the map view that also highlights trail information and photo stops that show actual digital photos of trail stops in winter and summer in an online virtual hike (fig. 20).

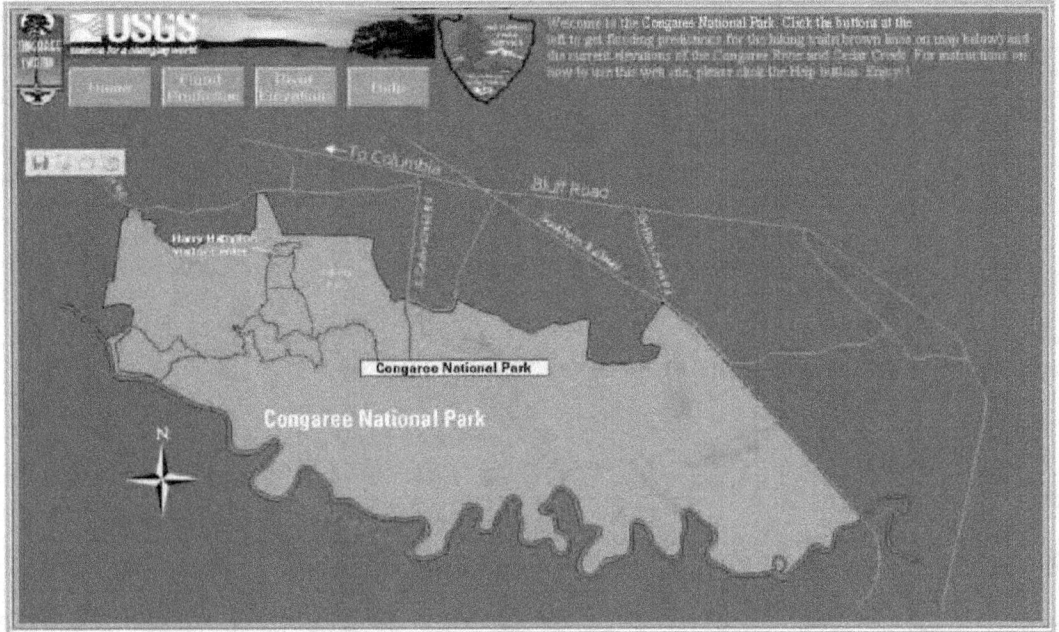

Figure 17. Graphic user interface of the Congaree National Park flood plain inundation model illustrating functional buttons for predicting current and 24-hour forecasts of flood conditions on park trails.

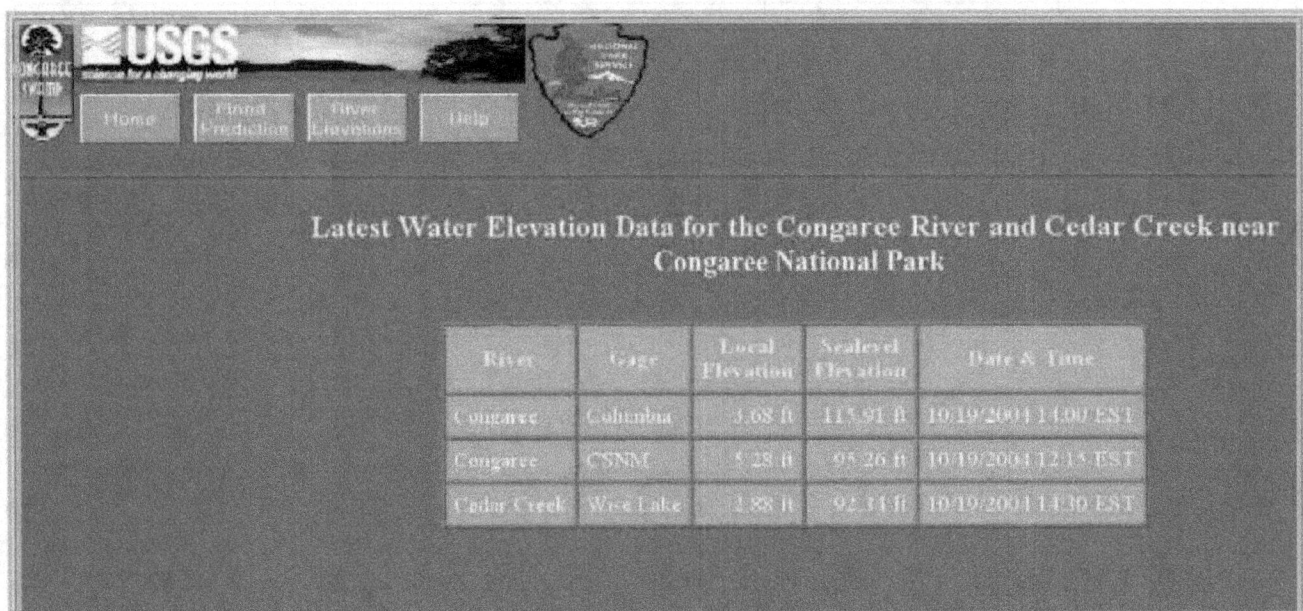

Figure 18. Graphic user interface of the Congaree National Park flood plain inundation model illustrating concurrent gage heights from the U.S. Geological Survey (USGS) National Water Information System Web site for the Congaree River at Columbia, S.C., and downstream park gages on the Congaree River and Cedar Creek.

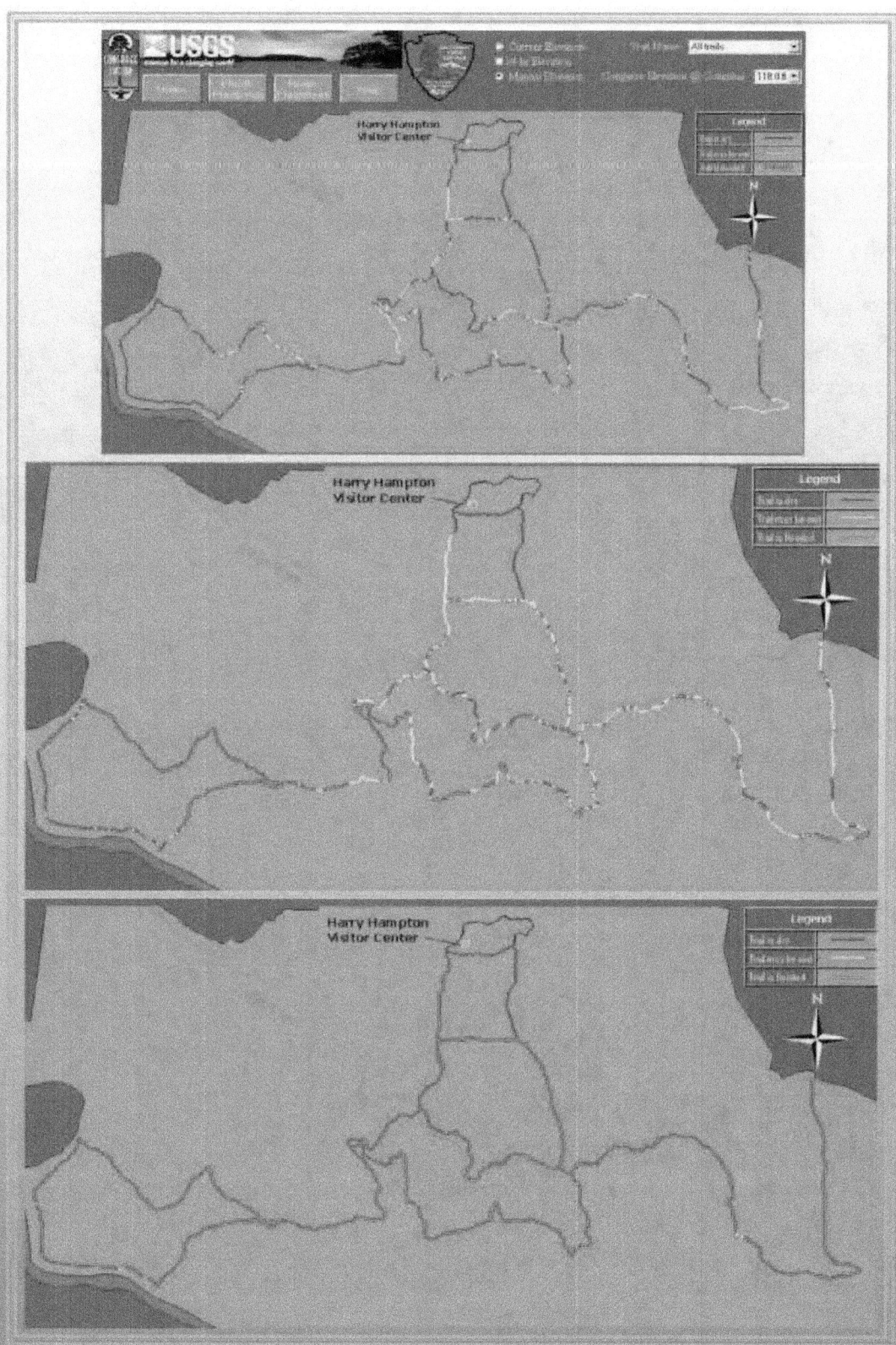

Figure 19. Illustrations of park trail condition (dry is indicated by brown, wet by yellow, and flooded by red) predicted by the Congaree National Park flood plain inundation model across the trail network at select stages of the Congaree River at Columbia, S.C.

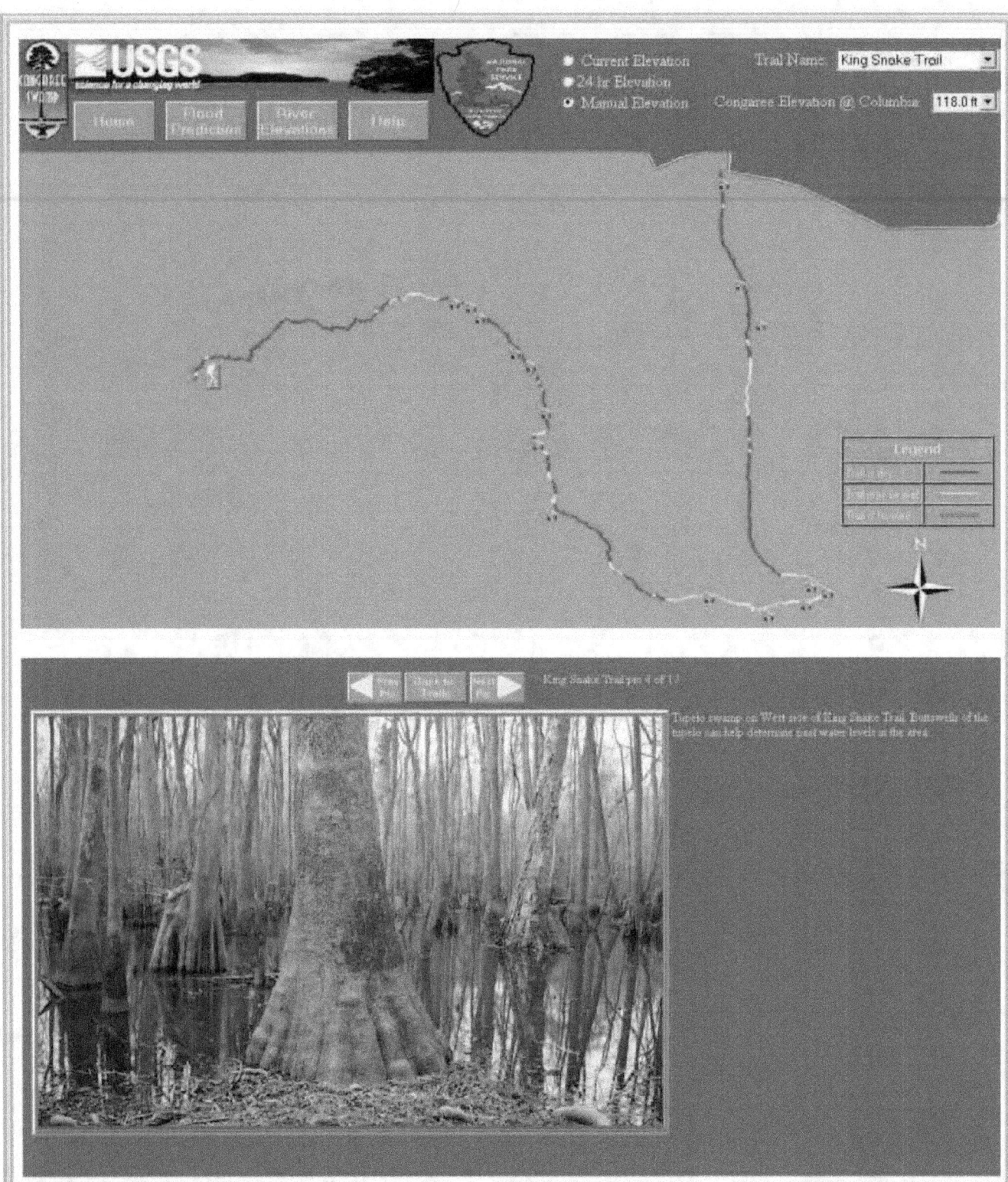

Figure 20.   Features of the Congaree National Park flood plain inundation model highlighting specific park trails of interest with an enlarged map view of trail information (top panel) and photo stops in winter and summer (bottom panel) in an online virtual hike format.

Tree-Ring Analysis

Forest Age and History

Tree cores had not heretofore been taken from Congaree National Park except to age select trees of loblolly pine and virgin specimens of baldcypress (Pederson and others, 1997; Laary Cushman and Joy Young, oral commun.). Remnant virgin-growth baldcypress trees are present in the park but were not cored for this study to avoid complications with growth analysis of millennial-aged trees. Results from this study showed that ages generally ranged from about 50 to 200 years old for the collective group of sampled trees and species (table 1). Most hardwood trees sampled were less than 100 years of age, though some individuals were nearly twice as old. Tree sizes were commonly more than 50 cm in diameter, with the largest individuals exceeding 1 m and a few as large as 1.5 m in diameter. Overall, the maximum growth rate for all species was fairly robust (greater than 1 cm/yr), excepting water tupelo. Species collections were generally on the higher elevations near full-bank elevation for backswamp zones on rich sandy, silt-loam soils that routinely receive continuous deposition following higher floods, excepting water tupelo and some baldcypress. Water tupelo was generally sampled from low-elevation sites along with some baldcypress collections where soil conditions are mostly saturated or semipermanently flooded from groundwater seepage, rainfall, or intermittent flood events.

Water tupelo sizes were much smaller than all other species with ages commonly between 100 and 200 years, even though some tupelo trees exceeded 300 years based on ring counts. Water tupelo specimens contained faint ring boundaries and suppressed ring series that complicated accurate dating and measurement. Suppressed ring series in water tupelo appeared to be quite abrupt and related to disturbance or stand development (crowding) rather than to age. Wind damage from hurricanes or thunderstorms may be primary causes leading to branch breakage and topping out of water tupelo canopies that match long suppressed ring series of 20 or more years before eventual recovery of detectable ring sizes and variation. In almost all cases, water tupelo were older than neighboring baldcypress of near equal size, which is perhaps related to baldcypress resistance to wind storms (Doyle and others, 1995; Conner and others, 2007; Doyle and others, 2007). The two primary tree species, loblolly pine and baldcypress, were sampled intensively across Congaree Swamp to construct growth chronologies for relating any effects of changing river stage that are due to stream regulation and operation of Saluda Dam.

Table 1.   Age and diameter ranges based on tree core analysis of select hardwood tree species at Congaree National Park.

Tree species (common name)	Age range, in years	Diameter range, in centimeters
Green ash	74–159	44–104
Laurel oak	70–129	48–104
Swamp chestnut oak	49–205	24–160
Sycamore	76–197	43–141
Water tupelo	97–170	49–63

Loblolly Pine Chronology Development and Productivity

Loblolly pine are common forest dominants in Congaree Swamp of appreciable age and size that can provide long-term growth records sufficient to span before and after operation of Saluda Dam and establishment of Lake Murray. Mean chronologies for pine specimens were constructed from seven sites or stands representing different hydrogeomorphic settings where flood history or hydroperiod was sufficiently different and unique to test for growth differences and relations. Three hydrogeomorphic settings were identified including upland sandhill (PinDry), flood plain seepage (PinWet), and flood plain full bank (PinBnk). Site names associated with each of these hydrogeomorphic classes are given along with age and diameter ranges of trees making up each chronology (table 2). Tree ages confirm that loblolly pine populations in Congaree Swamp are old growth up to 200 years old (table 2; Pederson and others, 1997). In all cases, sample trees are dominant and emergent canopy trees approaching 40 m in height based on actual ground measurements of fallen trees. This aging population of pines is subject to senescence and windthrow by tropical storms and other extreme wind events.

Mean growth chronologies of annual BAI were constructed from loblolly pine populations at seven sites within the park that were categorized into three hydrogeomorphic classes (fig. 21). Each chronology represents the common variance and mean growth by year for 10 or more trees and 20 or more cores per site. Results showed highly synchronous growth behavior year to year and over the long term but showed different ranges of productivity potential. The PinDry group and site is an upland sandhill environment within the park's bluff zone that has no influence of river flooding given that it is more than 9 m above Congaree Swamp. The wet flatwoods condition of this site is influenced by area rainfall and a sandy soil type lacking the soil quality and fertility to sustain high growth rates relative to flood plain soils of higher silt and clay composition. A similar site chronology and productivity ranging in annual BAI from 10 to 25 cm^2 are found among the PinWet group (at site HQA) located on organic soils within the seepage zone that remains more or less saturated year round from groundwater drainage. Other seepage zone pine populations sustained intermediate stemwood production rates between 20 and 70 cm^2, comparable to some PinBnk sites of nearly equal site quality. The PinBnk group sustained the highest levels of stemwood productivity, approaching 100 cm^2 for select years. Even though the range of stemwood productivity varies greatly with site, the temporal pattern of productivity change year to year and over the long term remained remarkably similar.

The year-to-year variation in tree-ring chronologies is usually attributed to climate influence and variability. Detrending filters are commonly used to reduce the low-frequency or long-term variation that is often associated with changes in stand density or is disturbance related. In this study, long-term variation in the growth record could also be the result of changing flood patterns as a function of dam construction and operation dating back to the 1930s. A 7-year running mean was applied to the mean chronologies to compare long-term changes and inflections in the growth record and the synchronicity or lack thereof between the different sites. Loblolly pine typically retains cohorts of needles from 5 to 7 years in age before being replaced with new needles. The combined needle sets contribute to tree productivity but to varying degrees on the basis of maturity. Developing needles of the current year and senescing needles may not add appreciably to stem growth potential as much as intermediate aged needles 2–4 years old do.

Results showed remarkable synchronicity of growth variation by time period among all sites, with some reduction in response amplitude with the least productive sites (fig. 22). The greatest differences and incongruity between sites

Table 2.   Site descriptions, site name abbreviations, and age and diameter ranges of loblolly pine tree core collections at Congaree National Park.

[Full names of sites are given in figure 9]

Hydrogeomorphic setting	Site name abbreviation	Age range, in years	Diameter range, in centimeters
PinDry	GAR	95–135	43–62
PinWet	EBW	161–198	70–114
PinWet	HQA	190–208	69–93
PinWet	HQB	152–181	89–123
PinBnk	PIP	127–172	81–112
PinBnk	SRV	132–193	83–131
PinBnk	WAR	159–169	82–103

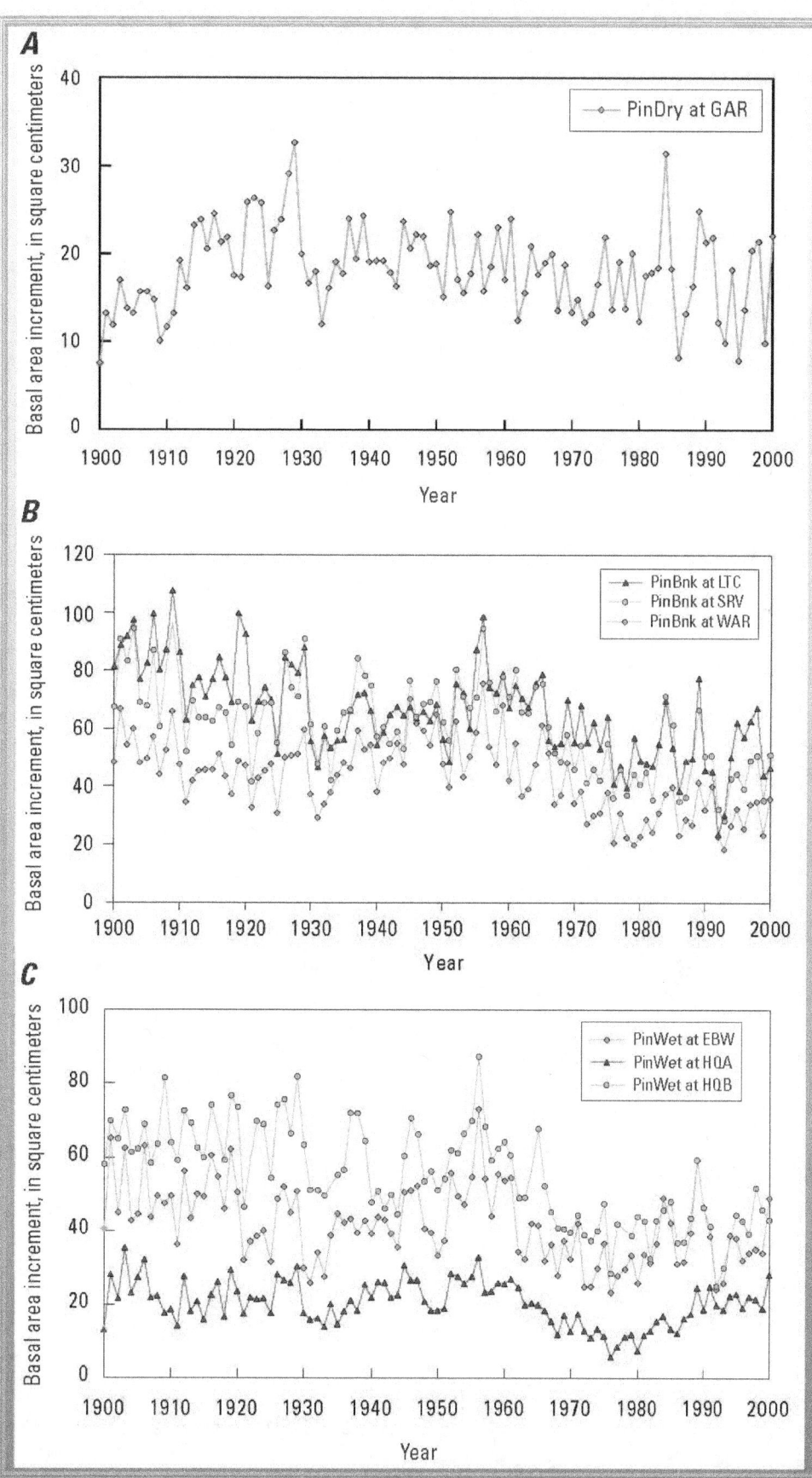

Figure 21. Mean growth chronologies of annual basal area increment (BAI) from loblolly pine populations at seven coring sites within Congaree National Park graphed by hydrogeomorphic association. *A,* Mean BAI chronology for upland sandhill (PinDry) at Garrick Road (GAR) site. *B,* Mean BAI chronologies for flood plain full bank (PinBnk) at Lower Toms Creek (LTC), Service Road (SRV), and West Access Road (WAR) sites. *C,* Mean BAI chronologies for flood plain seepage (PinWet) at Elevated Boardwalk (EBW), Headquarters A (HQA), and Headquarters B (HQB) sites.

occurred early in the record between young and mature chronologies until convergence was achieved during the mid-1910s. This result indicates that all chronologies are responding to an overriding influence, climate or flood regime, that is ubiquitous across the park flood plain and uplands, rather than to disturbance or land-use effects that are more likely to have occurred at different places and at different times. The synchronous rises and falls during the postdam era from 1935 to present do not support the likelihood of flood effects or other land-use effects as probable causes. Logging or high-grading activities can foster growth releases, but always over a short term of a few years, and usually result in threefold to fivefold increases in growth rate, neither of which are observed here. The relatively gradual and characteristic patterns of positive and negative growth inflections appear more climate related than dam or disturbance related. Long-term climate patterns of favorable or less favorable temperature or precipitation patterns have been associated with long-term growth variance.

Loblolly Pine Climate-Growth Relations

Division climate data of mean monthly temperature, precipitation, and Palmer Drought Severity Index (PDSI) were used to associate short- and long-term relations with these loblolly pine growth chronologies. The PDSI and precipitation data are highly intercorrelated because of the weighted use of precipitation to derive the PDSI. Temperature and precipitation are more independent of each other and can be used individually or together to test model fit for explaining growth as a function of climate. Single factor relations are illustrated here to demonstrate the degree to which certain climate parameters and data reductions did or did not correlate with loblolly pine growth over the last century. To determine whether growth is correlated with frequency of rainfall during the spring/summer growing season months (March–August), the monthly precipitation record was reduced by counting the number of months with above average rainfall for the period of record. Results showed a slight but poor correlation between precipitation frequency and growth of flood plain loblolly pine (PinBnk) by year (fig. 23A). There was, however, no discernible correlation with quantity of rainfall for the spring/summer growing season (fig. 23B). The results are the same if the annual record is averaged over a 7-year period to capture the long-term precipitation pattern; however, averaging the annual air temperature over a 7-year period including a 2-year lag explains more than 50 percent of the variation in mean loblolly pine growth (fig. 23C). The 2-year lag may be related to the maturity and function of intermediate-aged needles that contribute more to current growth than do current

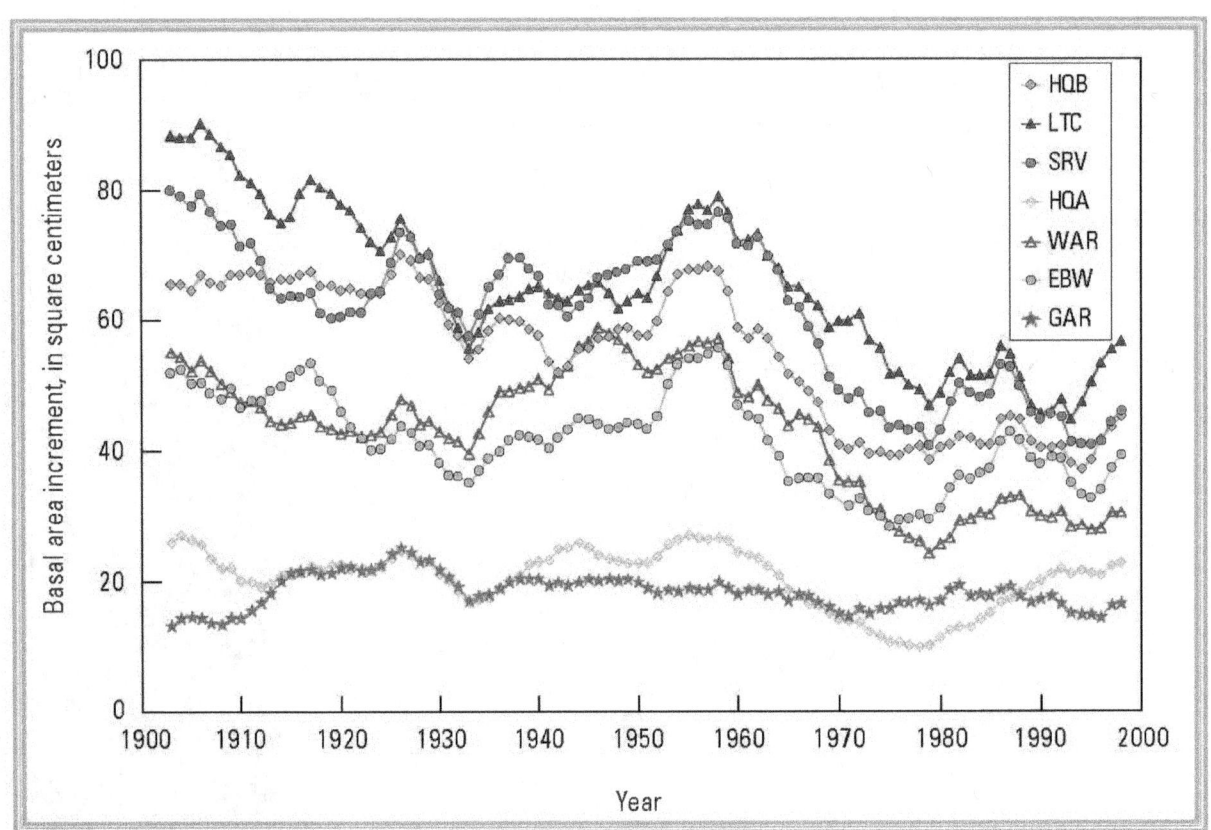

Figure 22. A 7-year running mean of basal area increment (BAI) chronologies among the different loblolly pine populations and sampling sites.

year needles. Warmer spring/summer temperature appears to foster greater growth potential for flood plain loblolly pine where available water at depth may not be limiting. Moreover, warmer temperatures and droughts may dry out some saturated soils which might otherwise limit loblolly pine growth potential. In contrast, there is no correlation of number of flood days by year for stage above 36.6 m at the Columbia gage of the Congaree River with flood plain growth of loblolly pine (fig. 23D).

Baldcypress Chronology Development and Productivity

Baldcypress were sampled in the park to develop growth chronologies and to determine any effects of changing climate and flood history. As a flood-tolerant species, baldcypress provides a contrast with loblolly pine, which is only moderately tolerant of flooding and thrives on relatively higher ground not subject to permanent flooding. Mean growth chronologies of baldcypress were constructed from six sites representing different hydrogeomorphic settings where flood history or hydroperiod were sufficiently different and unique to test for growth differences and relations. Two hydrogeomorphic settings were identified including riverbank (CypDry) and backswamp (CypWet) environments of higher and lower elevations and shorter and longer hydroperiods, respectively. Site designations associated with each of these

hydrogeomorphic classes are given along with age and diameter ranges of trees making up each chronology (table 3). Tree ages confirmed that baldcypress populations cored for this study are old growth, with some approaching 300 years old. Trees sampled along riverbank (CypDry) settings were generally of younger cohorts and codominant canopy trees with other hardwood species more typical of seasonally flooded forests. Trees sampled in backswamp environments included low-elevation sites dominated by baldcypress and its common associate water tupelo, known to persist in semipermanently flooded forests. The size range of sampled trees in the CypWet sites was generally smaller for the same relative age, indicative of slower growth rates typical of flooded versus drained conditions.

Six growth chronologies of annual BAI were constructed from baldcypress sites within Congaree Swamp from riverbank (CypDry) and backswamp (CypWet) settings (fig. 24). Chronology comparisons showed highly synchronous growth behavior year to year and over the long term but showed different ranges of productivity potential by site condition. The CypDry group occupies riverbank environments that flood infrequently and only when river flow nears peak flood stages. Mean chronologies for the two groups showed a difference in productivity range of 10–40 cm^2 BAI for the CypWet group in contrast to 20–60 cm^2 BAI for the CypDry group. Other tree growth studies have shown that baldcypress grows better on aerated drained soils than in anaerobically saturated or deeply flooded sites. Similar

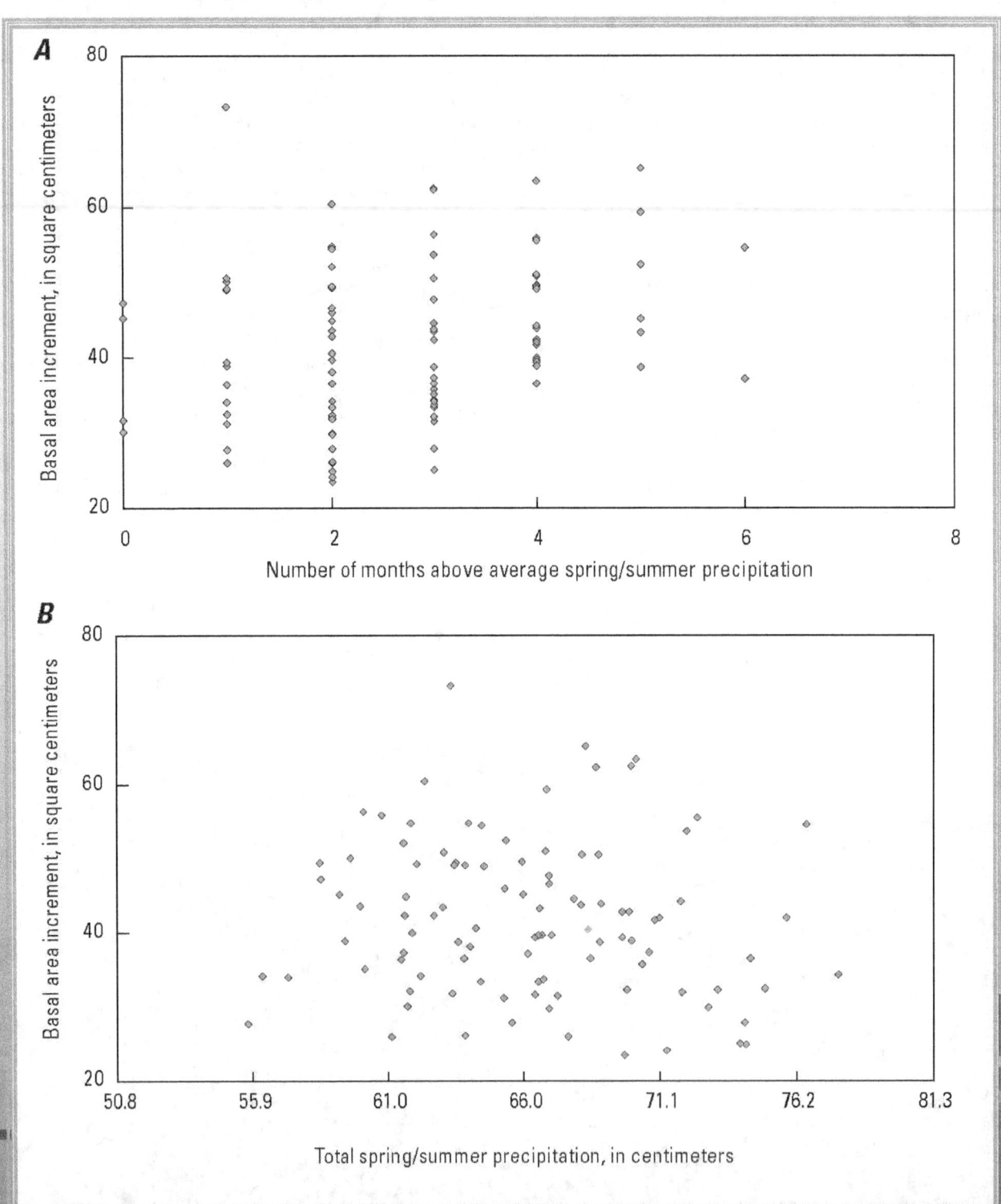

Figure 23. Relation between mean annual basal area increment (BAI) of loblolly pine growth with various climate and hydrology parameters. *A*, Growth related to number of months of above average spring/summer (March–August) precipitation. *B*, Growth related to total precipitation for spring/summer months (March–August). *C*, A 7-year growth period and temperature relation with a 2-year time lag offset indicating greater growth potential under warmer growing season temperatures. *D*, Growth related to number of flood days by year for stage above 36.6 m at the Columbia, S.C., gage.

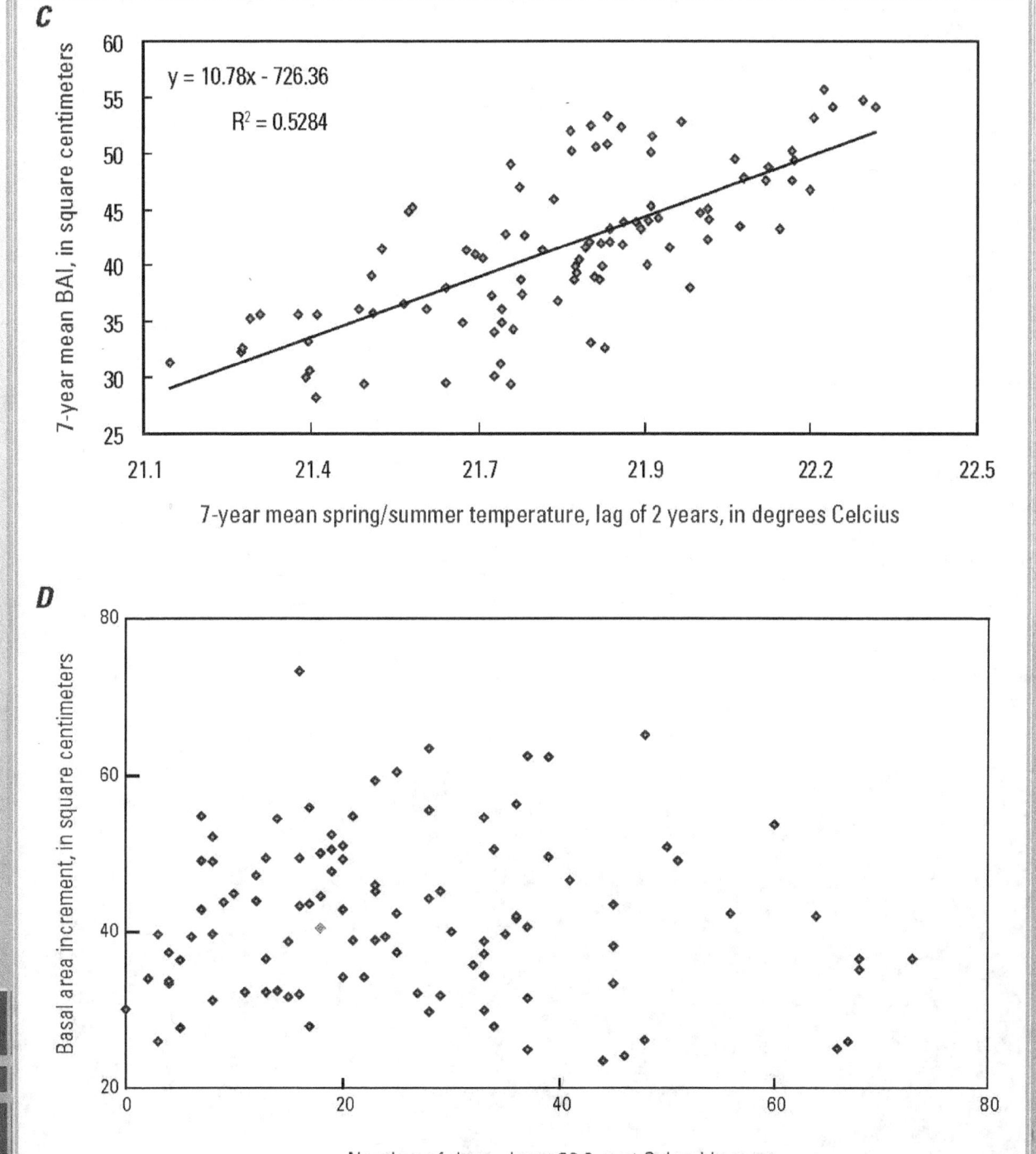

C

$y = 10.78x - 726.36$

$R^2 = 0.5284$

7-year mean BAI, in square centimeters

7-year mean spring/summer temperature, lag of 2 years, in degrees Celcius

D

Basal area increment, in square centimeters

Number of days above 36.6 m at Columbia gage

Table 3.   Site descriptions, site name abbreviations, and age and diameter ranges of baldcypress tree core collections at Congaree National Park.

[Full names of sites are given in figure 9]

Hydrogeomorphic setting	Site name abbreviations	Age range, in years	Diameter range, in centimeters
CypDry	HRS	112–115	54–115
CypDry	LCC	109–162	60–102
CypDry	VCC	106–235	56–107
CypWet	BWK	172–295	53–109
CypWet	LTC	119–208	45–51
CypWet	TCF	69–195	45–88

to the loblolly pine chronologies there is a high degree of synchronicity of year-to-year variation, indicating that trees under wet or dry settings are responding to similar climate or environmental factors. Contrasting the two group chronologies demonstrated that the initial slope is a product of younger CypDry trees yet to establish maturity compared with the older set of CypWet trees, which achieved convergence by 1920 and then had level growth to 1990 followed by a growth release after Hurricane Hugo (1989) damage to neighboring hardwood trees along the river's edge (fig. 25).

Baldcypress Climate-Growth Relations

A 7-year running mean was derived from the mean chronologies to compare long-term changes and inflections in the growth record and the synchronicity or lack thereof between the different hydrogeomorphic groups. Results demonstrated that the collective baldcypress chronologies also exhibit remarkable synchronicity between sites and groups, CypDry and CypWet, with the greatest difference in the range of productivity and a post-1989 hurricane effect (fig. 26). This result indicates that all chronologies are responding

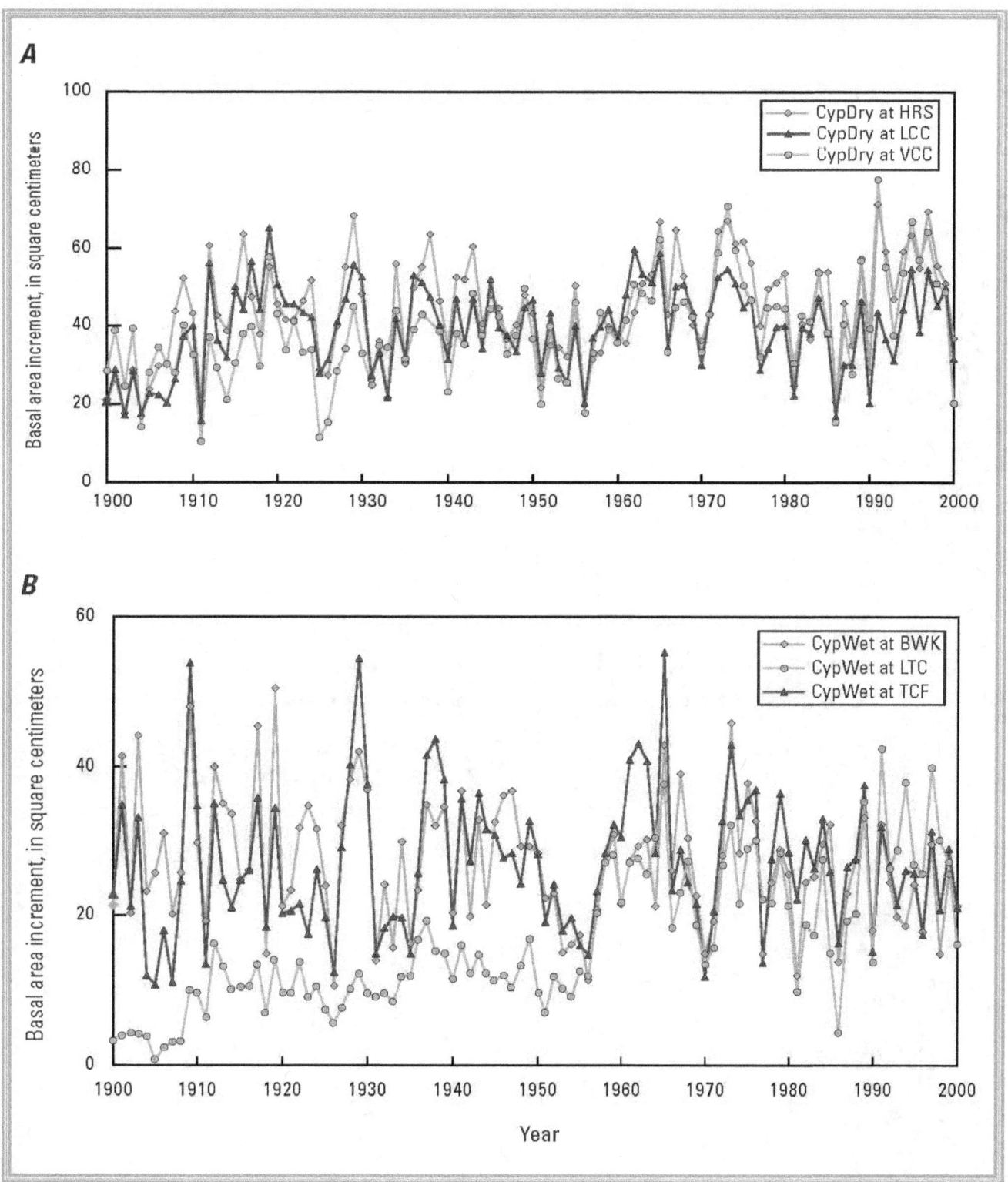

Figure 24. Mean basal area increment (BAI) growth chronologies of baldcypress populations within Congaree National Park by hydrogeomorphic association. *A*, Riverbank baldcypress populations (CypDry) at sites Horsepen (HRS), Lower Cedar Creek (LCC), and Virgin Cedar Creek (VCC). *B*, Backswamp baldcypress populations (CypWet) at sites Boardwalk (BWK), Lower Toms Creek (LTC), and Toms Creek flood plain (TCF).

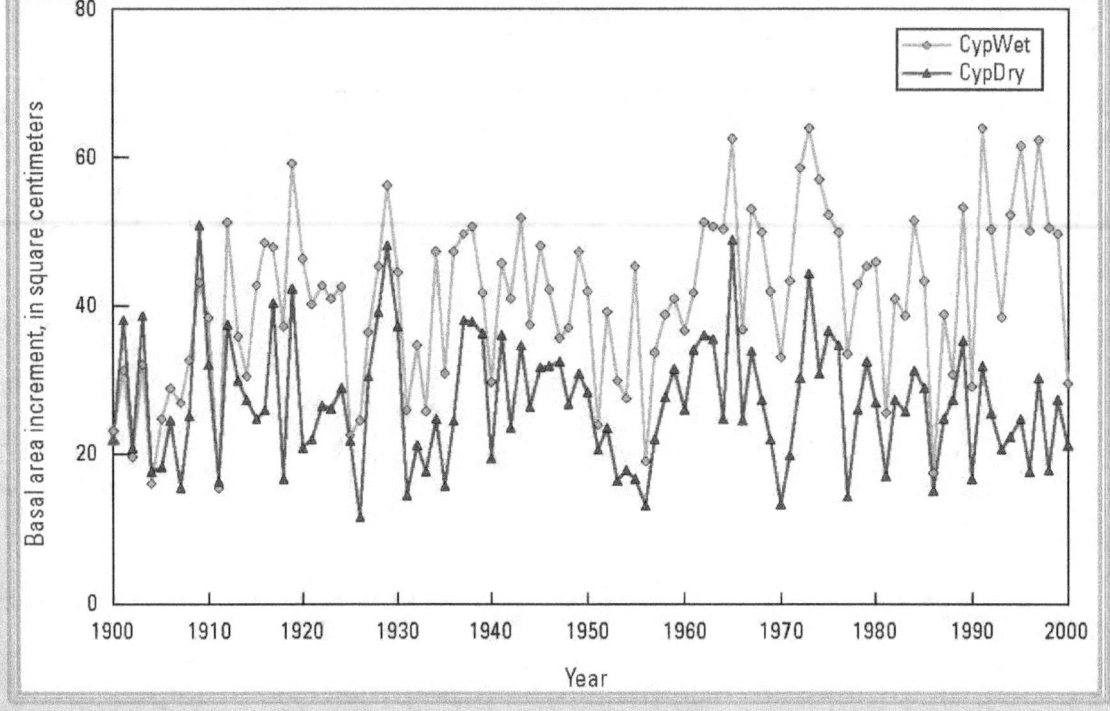

Figure 25. Mean basal area increment (BAI) growth chronologies of baldcypress by hydrogeomorphic groupings contrasting productivity of riverbank (CypDry) sites versus backswamp (CypWet) sites.

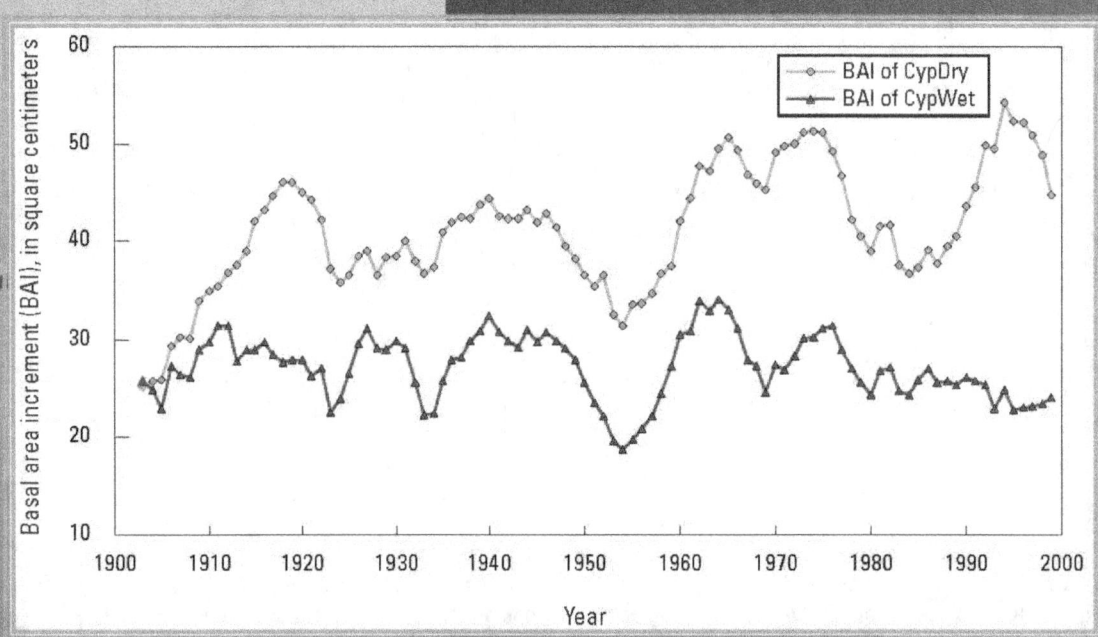

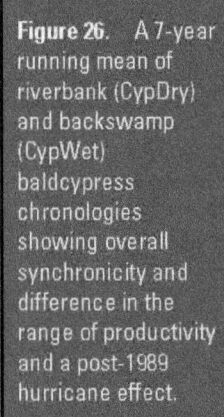

Figure 26. A 7-year running mean of riverbank (CypDry) and backswamp (CypWet) baldcypress chronologies showing overall synchronicity and difference in the range of productivity and a post-1989 hurricane effect.

to an overriding influence, climate or flood regime, that is ubiquitous across Congaree Swamp rather than to disturbance or land-use effects that are more likely to have occurred at different places and at different times. The synchronous rises and falls during the postdam era from 1935 to present do not support the likelihood of flood effects or other land-use effects as probable causes, a result that is similar to that of the loblolly pine analysis. Furthermore, there are differences in species productivity and pattern between loblolly pine and baldcypress chronologies that indicate different sensitivities to different climate variables.

Riverbank (CypDry) chronologies might be expected to be more sensitive to the frequency of precipitation events or high floods given the drained conditions and high percolation of the largely sandy soils typical of depositional levee environments; however, there was no apparent correlation of baldcypress growth corresponding to number of flood days above 36.6 m at the Columbia gage of the Congaree River (fig. 27A). There was a slight but poor correlation of mean spring/summer temperature, indicating that cooler temperatures enhance growth potential or account for increasing rainfall and cloudy days (fig. 27B). Similarly, there was a weak correlation of increasing spring/summer precipitation with greater growth potential (fig. 27C); however, correlating the 7-year running average of spring/summer PDSI (surrogate precipitation) with baldcypress growth explained more than 56 percent of the variation in growth (fig. 27D). Other tree-ring studies of

baldcypress purport the importance of spring precipitation on species growth (Stahle and others, 1985, 1988; Stahle and Cleaveland, 1992, 1994; Cleaveland, 2000).

Saluda Dam Effects on River Stage and Tree Growth

Saluda Dam was completed in the early 1930s to create Lake Murray from the Saluda River near its confluence of the Broad River and headwaters of the Congaree River. Analysis of stage records for the Congaree River at Columbia dating back to 1892 indicated dramatic changes in the number of flood days above low stage at 35.3 m (mean sea level) following dam construction and operation (fig. 28). Gage relations showed that floodwaters circulate into Congaree Swamp when river stage at Columbia exceeds 36.6 m (mean sea level), flooding some of the park trail system and trees enough to potentially affect visitor safety and tree growth. Records of flooding and growth every 15 years prior to (predam) and following (postdam) dam operation were summed to test for differences in tree growth by species and hydrogeomorphic setting. Fifteen years was determined to be a sufficiently long period to allow for a flooding effect and to moderate the combination of wet and dry years of climate and flooding on growth to effectively determine an incremental

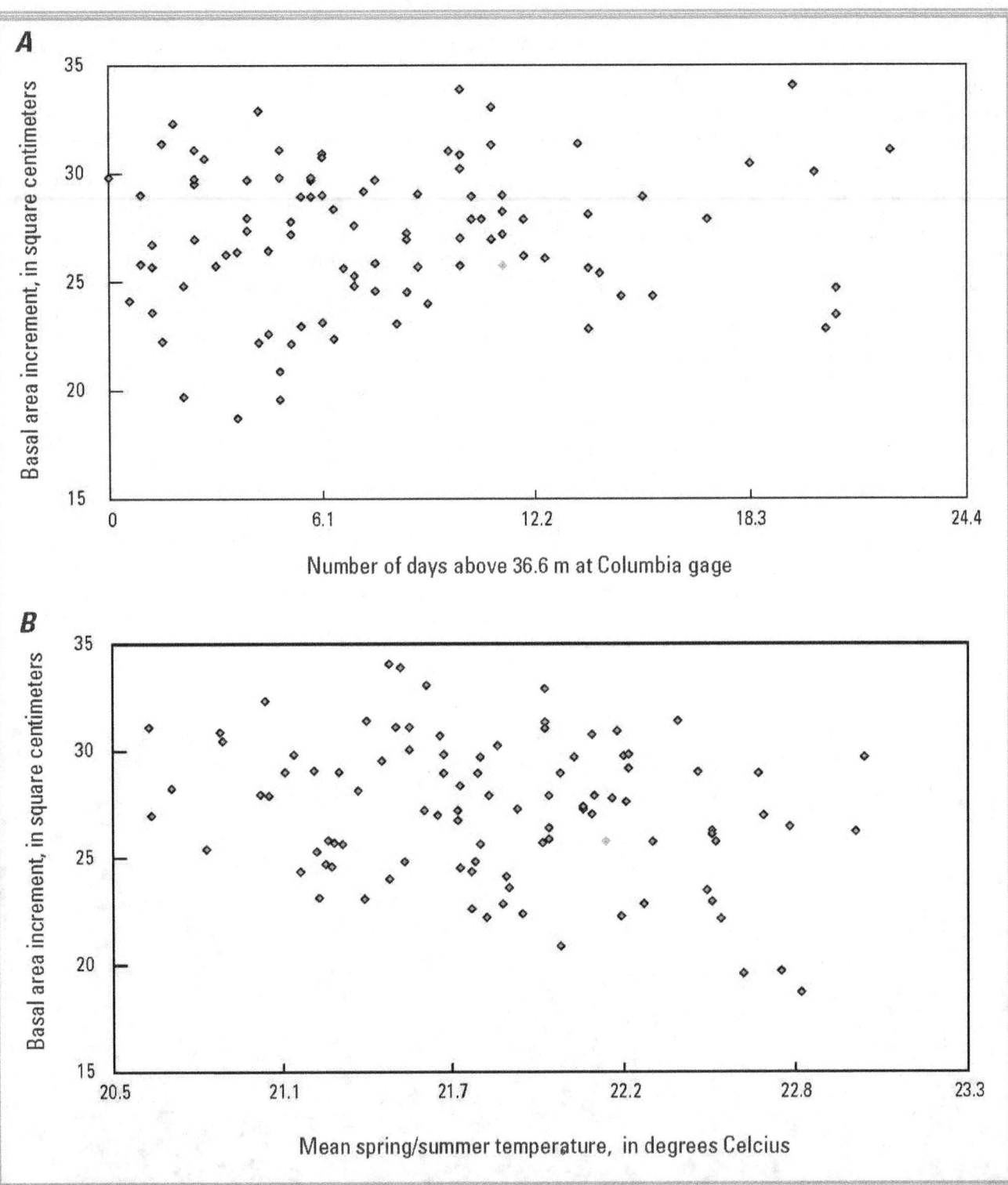

Figure 27.   Relation between mean annual basal area increment (BAI) of riverbank baldcypress growth with various climate and hydrology parameters. *A*, Growth related to number of flood days by year for stage above 36.6 m at the Columbia, S.C., gage. *B*, Growth related to mean temperature for spring/summer months (March–August). *C*, Growth related to total precipitation for spring/summer months (March–August). *D*, A 7-year growth period and spring/summer PDSI relation indicating an increase of tree growth with increasing wetness.

C

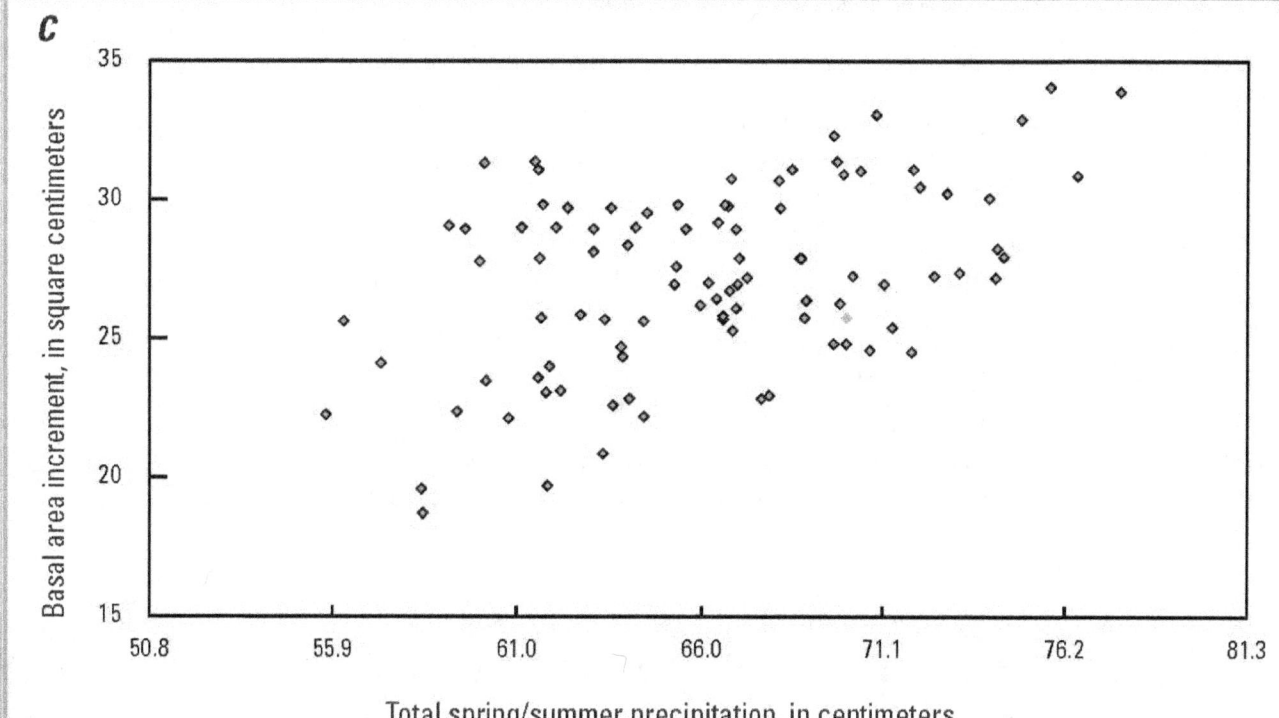

Total spring/summer precipitation, in centimeters

D

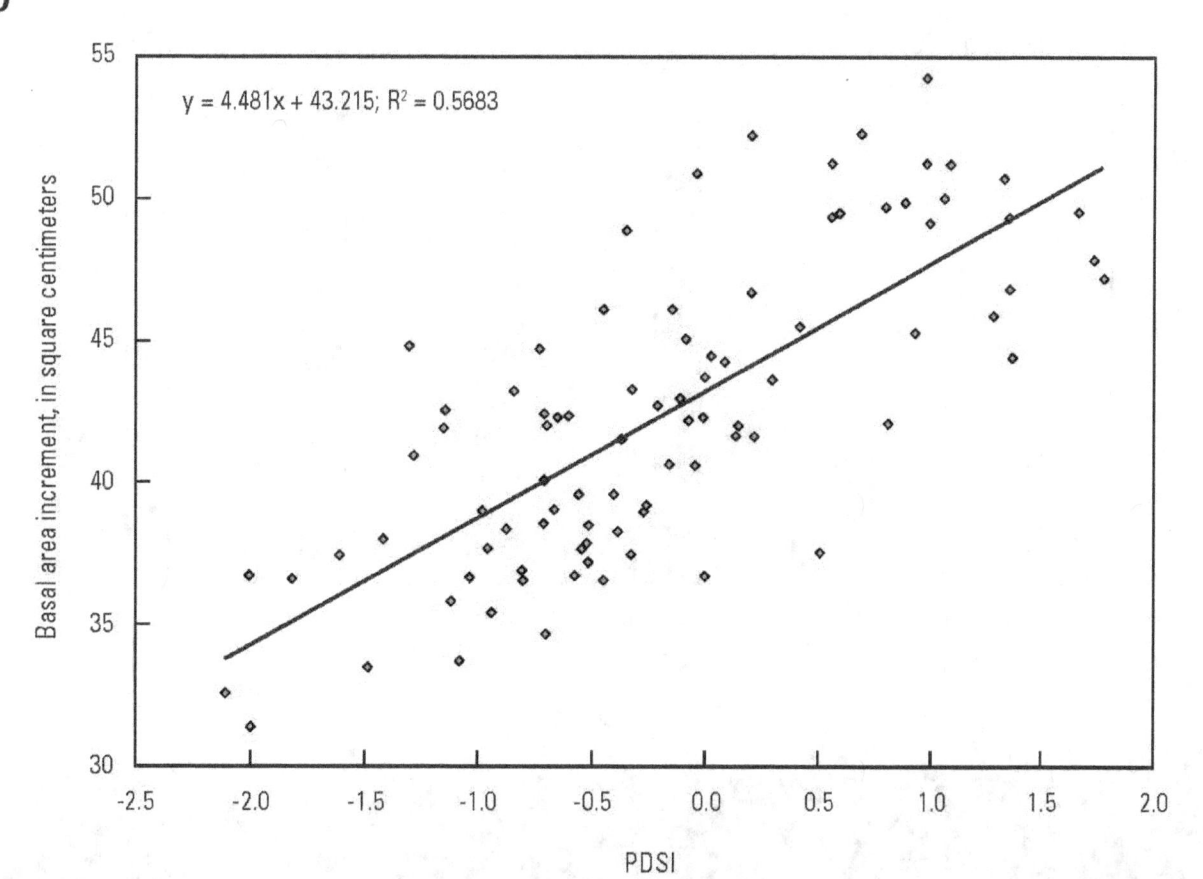

PDSI

or sustained effect of change in river stage from predam and postdam conditions.

A two-way analysis of variation (ANOVA) was used to test for differences in tree growth by species and hydrogeomorphic setting between successive periods prior to dam construction (1900–29) and in the postdam operating period (1935–79) (table 4). There were no differences between sampling periods, before or after operation of the dam, that had any effect on loblolly pine or baldcypress species on wet or dry sites (fig. 29). There were some minor differences mainly between species of higher and lower growth deviation among the postdam periods that are due to lower than normal spring/summer precipitation, negatively affecting baldcypress, and warmer than normal spring/summer temperatures, fostering greater loblolly pine growth (table 4). Because wet sites reduced species productivity for both loblolly pine and baldcypress in contrast to drained sites, it would be inconsistent to expect that increasing flood conditions would do likewise. Only climate variations and correlations suitably explain the divergent postdam growth differences between species, indicating that the increased daily stage from dam releases was not sufficient to suppress or augment forest growth beyond other climatic influences.

Summary

A forest growth and flood plain hydrology study was conducted in Congaree National Park, S.C., to determine the flood relations of backswamp forests and park trails as influenced by river stage and flood plain elevation by utilizing an integrated field and modeling approach. Water level gages were distributed across the length and width of "Congaree

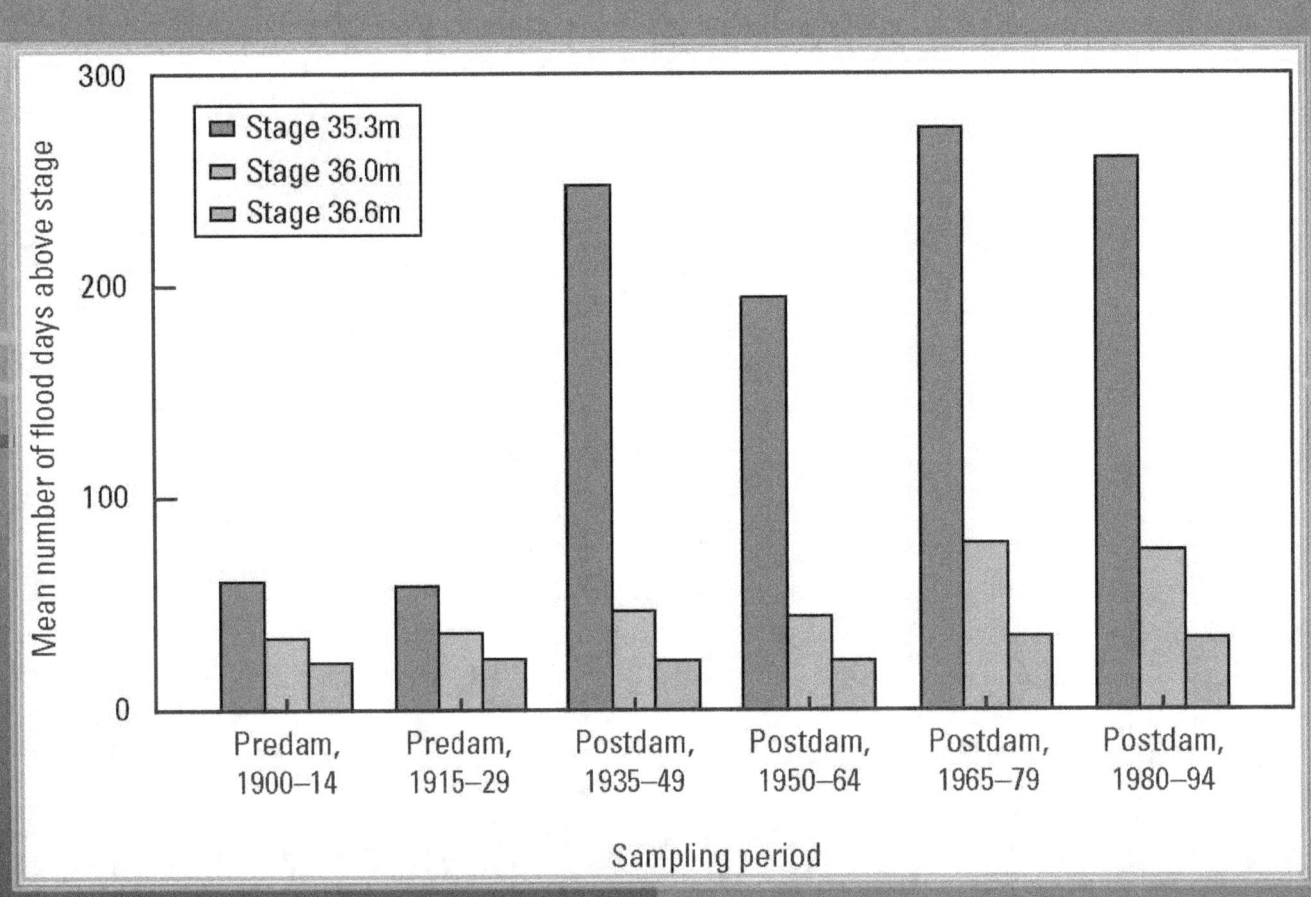

Figure 28.   The number of flood days above select stages at 35.3 m, 36.0 m, and 36.6 m mean sea level for the Congaree River at Columbia, S.C., for predam and postdam periods spanning 15 years each dating from 1900 to 1994 and illustrating a marked increase in low flow conditions with dam operation.

Table 4.   Contrasts of mean annual basal area increment (BAI, in square centimeters) over a 15-year period for five successive periods before (predam) and after (postdam) construction and operation of the Saluda Dam near Columbia, S.C.

[Letters (a–h) signify statistical contrast by species groupings such that values with the same letters are not significantly different from one another]

Species group	Predam 1900–14	Predam 1915–29	Postdam 1935–49	Postdam 1950–64	Postdam 1965–79
PinDry	71 a	63 b	64 b	66 b	47 b
PinWet	46 c	46 c	41 c	45 c	29 d
CypDry	30 e	42 fg	42 fg	38 eg	48 f
CypWet	28 h	28 h	30 h	25 h	29 h

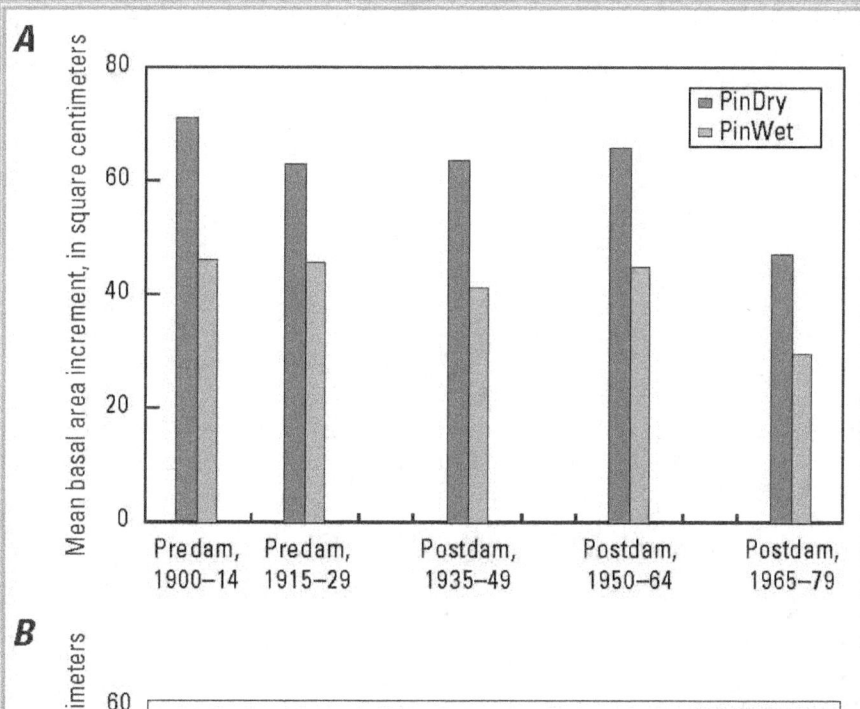

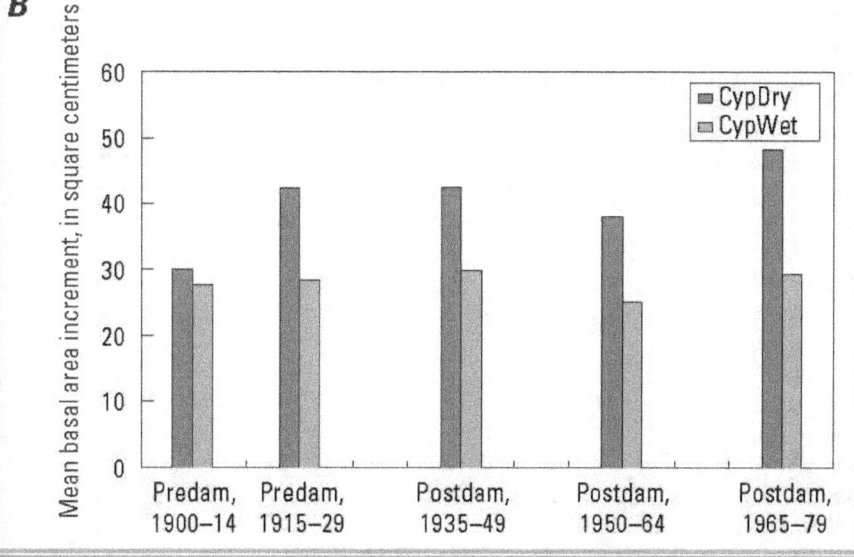

Figure 29.   Mean annual basal area increment (BAI) of loblolly pine and baldcypress populations for different predam and postdam periods on more (PinWet, CypWet) or less (PinDry, CypDry) flooded sites in Congaree National Park.

Swamp" (the flood plain portion of the park) to capture the lag and peak flood relations to river stage. A severe and prolonged drought at the study start in 2001 continued into 2002 before water levels were monitored over a 4-year period from 2002 to 2006. Historical water level stage and discharge data from the Congaree River were collated and digitized from published sources and U.S. Geological Survey (USGS) archives to obtain long-term daily averages for an upstream gage at Columbia, S.C. Hydrological studies of the Congaree River demonstrated that the magnitude and frequency of floods had been greatly reduced following construction of Saluda Dam (Whetstone, 1982; Patterson and others, 1985); however, daily stage was shown to actually increase rather than decrease after 1934 as a result of dam operation. Flood volumes associated with the Saluda River are effectively stored behind Saluda Dam and released in operational pulses days and weeks later for hydropower.

Elevation surveys of ground surface were completed for all park trails and for additional circuits of roads and boundaries to create a digital elevation model for predicting inundation patterns and periods from floods. Regression models were applied to establish time lags and stage relations between gages at Columbia and in the upper, middle, and lower reaches of the Congaree River and backswamp within the park. Flood relations among backswamp gages showed that the retention and recession behavior between flood plain reaches was longer in the lower reach than in the upper and middle reaches of Congaree Swamp. Mathematical functions were developed to define the flooding envelope for position on the landscape gradient when the soil surface is either predictably wet or dry in relation to river stage. A Web-based flood plain inundation model was developed to predict critical river stages and potential inundation of hiking trails on a real-time basis and to allow the flood inundation model to forecast the 24-hour flood condition on the trail network within the park. Park officials have used the model to understand the process and pattern of trail flooding and to advise park visitors of current and advanced flood hazards.

Tree-ring analysis was used to evaluate the effects of flood events and flood history on forest resources at Congaree National Park. Tree core samples were collected from populations of loblolly pine (*Pinus taeda*), baldcypress (*Taxodium distichum*), water tupelo (*Nyssa aquatica*), green ash (*Fraxinus pennslyvanica*), laurel oak (*Quercus laurifolia*), swamp chestnut oak (*Quercus michauxii*), and sycamore (*Plantanus occidentalis*) within Congaree Swamp in short- and long-retention flood sites. Findings showed that all loblolly pine trees and nearly all baldcypress collections for this study are postsettlement and old growth, dating from 100 to 300 years in age. Remnant virgin-growth baldcypress trees are present in the park but were not cored for this study to avoid complications with growth analysis of millennial-aged trees. Hardwood species demonstrated robust growth rates and relatively young cohorts, indicative of past logging activity and disturbance history. Growth chronologies of loblolly pine and baldcypress collections exhibited positive and negative

inflections over the last century that corresponded with macroclimate patterns and residual effects of Hurricane Hugo (1989). Water level data demonstrated that operations of the Saluda Dam (post-1934) have increased average daily stage in the Congaree River and flood plain, whereas tree-ring data provided no evidence of long-term change or interannual effect in forest productivity related to dam operation or flood history. Stemwood production on average was lower for trees and species on sites with longer flood retention and hydroperiod, affected more by groundwater seepage or site elevation than by fluctuating river stage or floods. Overall, forest growth is fairly robust for all tree species and controlled largely by macroclimatic conditions over the long term, and to a limited degree in the short term, by intermittent disturbance, either logging or hurricane impact such as canopy tree removal and openings. Forest maturity and increasing canopy roughness in Congaree Swamp may sustain or increase forest turnover of canopy trees in coming years. New forest studies should focus on species recruitment in gaps and on the age and vigor of subcanopy trees to determine whether flood patterns have shaped the contemporary species distribution and regeneration that will shape future forests.

Acknowledgments

This study was funded under the joint U.S. Geological Survey and National Park Service Natural Resources Preservation Program. The author is grateful to Bobbi Simpson, former Natural Resource Manager, and Martha Bogle, former Superintendent, Congaree National Park, for promoting the need, vision, and logistics in support of this effort. The author is indebted to many people who contributed invaluable assistance with field work and model development including Jason Sullivan, Rick Putnam, Andy From, Marcus Melder, Ben Handley, Michael Cooper, and Kelia Fontenot. William Conner, Chris Swarzenski, Scott Zengel, Rassa Dale, and park staff provided valuable technical and editorial reviews. Guy Frantello provided land and river access across private lands managed under the Sanbar Hunting Club to remote park areas and water level recorders important to the success of this study. Logistical assistance was provided by park staff including Bill Hulslander, Theresa Yednock, and others for incidental help to aid field forays.

References

Allen, B.P., Pauley, E.F., and Sharitz, R.R., 1997, Hurricane impacts on liana populations in an old-growth southeastern bottomland forest: Journal of the Torrey Botanical Society, v. 124, p. 34–42.

Allen, B.P., and Sharitz, R.R., 1999, Post-hurricane vegetation dynamics in old-growth forests of the Congaree Swamp National Monument, *in* On the frontiers of conservation: Hancock, Mich., George Wright Society Bulletin, p. 306–312.

Bridges, E.L., and Orzell, S.L., 1989, Longleaf pine communities of the West Gulf Coastal Plain: Natural Areas Journal, v. 9, p. 246–263.

Brown, S., 1981, A comparison of the structure, primary productivity, and transpiration of cypress ecosystems in Florida: Ecological Monographs, v. 51, p. 403–427.

Carter, V., 1986, An overview of the hydrologic concerns related to wetlands in the United States: Journal of Applied Ecology, v. 21, p. 1041–1057.

Cleaveland, M.K., 2000, A 963-year reconstruction of summer streamflow in the White River, Arkansas, USA, from tree-rings: Holocene, v. 10, p. 33–41.

Conner, W.H., and Day, J.W., Jr., 1992, Diameter growth of *Taxodium distichum* (L.) Rich. and *Nyssa aquatica* L. from 1979-1985 in four Louisiana swamp stands: American Midland Naturalist, v. 127, p. 290–299.

Conner, W.H., and Flynn, K., 1989, Growth and survival of baldcypress (*Taxodium distichum*) planted across a flooding gradient in a Louisiana bottomland hardwood forest: Wetlands, v. 9, p. 207–217.

Conner, W.H., Krauss, K.W., and Doyle, T.W., 2007, Ecology of tidal freshwater forests in coastal deltaic Louisiana and northeastern South Carolina, *in* Conner, W.H., Doyle, T.W, and Krauss, K.W., eds., Ecology of tidal freshwater forested wetlands of the Southeastern United States: New York, Springer, p. 223–254.

Conrads, P.A., Feaster, T.D., and Harrelson, L.G., 2008, The effects of the Saluda Dam on the surface-water and ground-water hydrology of the Congaree National Park flood plain, South Carolina: U.S. Geological Survey Scientific Investigations Report 2008–5170, 58 p., available online at http://pubs.water.usgs.gov/sir2008–5170.

Cook, E.R., Glitzenstein, J.S., Krusic, P.J., and Harcombe, P.A., 2001, Identifying functional groups of trees in West Gulf Coast forests (USA)—a tree ring approach: Ecological Applications, v. 11, p. 883–903.

Darst, M.R., and Light, H.M., 2008, Drier forest composition associated with hydrologic change in the Apalachicola River floodplain, Florida: U.S. Geological Survey Scientific Investigations Report 2008–5062, 81 p. plus 12 apps.

Day, R.H., Doyle, T.W., and Dale, R.O., 2006, Effects of hydrology, substrate, and nutrients on seedling growth of *Taxodium distichum* and *Salix nigra*: Environmental and Experimental Botany, v. 55, p. 163–174.

Dicke, S.G., and Toliver, J.R., 1990, Growth and development of bald-cypress/water tupelo stands under continuous versus seasonal flooding: Forest Ecology and Management, v. 33/34, p. 523–530.

Doyle, T.W., Conner, W.H., Ratard, M., and Inabinette, L.W., 2007, Assessing the impact of tidal flooding and salinity on long-term growth of baldcypress under changing climate and riverflow, *in* Conner, W.H., Doyle, T.W, and Krauss, K.W., eds., Ecology of tidal freshwater forested wetlands of the Southeastern United States: New York, Springer, p. 411–446.

Doyle, T.W., and Girod, G., 1997, The frequency and intensity of Atlantic hurricanes and their influence on the structure of south Florida mangrove communities, *in* Diaz, H., and Pulwarty, R., eds., Hurricanes, climatic change and socioeconomic impacts—a current perspective: New York, Westview Press, p. 111–128.

Doyle, T.W., and Gorham, L.E., 1996, Detecting hurricane impact and recovery from tree rings, *in* Dean, Meko, and Swetnam, eds., Tree rings, environment, and humanity: Tucson, Ariz., Radiocarbon, p. 405–412.

Doyle, T.W., Keeland, B.D., Gorham, L.E., and Johnson, D.J., 1995, Structural impact of Hurricane Andrew on forested wetlands of the Atchafalaya Basin in coastal Louisiana: Journal of Coastal Research, v. 18, p. 354–364.

Fritts, H.C., 1976, Tree rings and climate: London, Academic Press.

Fritts, H.C., and Swetnam, T.W., 1989, Dendroecology—a tool for evaluating variations in past and present forest environments: Advances in Ecological Research, v. 19, p. 111–188.

Gaddy, L.L, 1977, Notes on the flora of the Congaree River floodplain, Richland County, South Carolina: Castanea, v. 42, p. 103–106.

Gardner, L.R., Michener, W.K., Blood, E.R., Williams, T.M., Lipscomb, D.J., and Jefferson, W.H., 1991, Ecological impact of Hurricane Hugo—salinization of a coastal forest: Journal of Coastal Research, v. 8, p. 301–317.

Gresham, C.A., Williams, T.M., and Linscomb, D.J., 1991, Hurricane Hugo wind damage to Southeastern U.S. coastal forest tree species: Biotropica, v. 44, p. 238–246.

Harcombe, P.A., Hall, R.B.W., Glitzenstein, J.S., Cook, E.S., Krusic, D.P., Fulton, M., and Streng, D.R., 1998, Sensitivity of Gulf Coast forests to climate change, *in* Guntenspergen, G.R., and Vairin, B.A., eds., Vulnerability of coastal wetlands in the Southeastern United States—climate change research results, 1992–97: Biological Science Report USGS/BRD/BSR—1998-0002, p. 45–66.

Hesse, I.D., Doyle, T.W., and Day, J.W., 1998, Long-term growth enhancement of baldcypress (*Taxodium distichum* (L.) Rich.) from municipal wastewater application: Environmental Management, v. 22, p. 119–127.

Hook, D.D., Buford, M.A., and Williams, T.M., 1991, Impact of Hurricane Hugo on the South Carolina coastal plain forest: Journal of Coastal Research, v. 8, p. 291–300.

Jones, R.H., 1997, Status and habitat of big trees in Congaree Swamp National Monument: Castanea, v. 62, p. 22–31.

Keeland, B.D., 1994, The effects of hydrologic regime on diameter growth of three wetland tree species of the Southeastern USA: Athens, University of Georgia, Ph.D. dissertation.

Lugo, A.E., and Brown, S.L., 1984, The Oklawaha River forested wetlands and their response to chronic flooding, *in* Ewel, K.C., and Odum, H.T., eds., Cypress swamps: Gainesville, University of Florida Press, p. 365–371.

Marks, P.L., and Harcombe, P.A., 1981, Forest vegetation of the Big Thicket, southeast Texas: Ecological Monographs, v. 51, p. 287–305.

Megonigal, P.J., and Day, F.P., 1992, Effects of flooding on root and shoot production of bald cypress in large experimental enclosures: Ecology, v. 73, p. 1182–1193.

Mitsch, W.J., and Gosselink, J.G., 1993, Wetlands (2d ed.): New York, Van Norstrand Reinhold.

Palmer, W.C., 1965, Meteorological drought. Research Paper No. 45: Washington, D.C., U.S. Weather Bureau, National Oceanic and Atmospheric Administration, Library and Information Services Division.

Palta, M.M., 2005, Changes in diameter growth of *Taxodium distichum* (l.) Rich in response to flow alterations in the Savannah River: Athens, University of Georgia, Ph.D. dissertation.

Patterson, G.G., Speiran, G.K., and Whetstone, B.H., 1985, Hydrology and its effect on distribution of vegetation in Congaree Swamp National Monument, South Carolina: Columbia, S.C., U.S. Geological Survey Water-Resources Investigations Report 85–4256.

Pederson, N.A., Jones, R.H., and Sharitz, R.R., 1997, Age structure and possible origins of old Pinus taeda stands in a flood plain forest: Journal of the Torrey Botanical Society, v. 124, p. 111–123.

Public Law 94–545, 1976, Congaree Swamp National Monument, S.C. Establishment. 90 STAT. 2517, 16 USC 431.

Putz, F.E., and Sharitz, R.R., 1991, Hurricane damage to old-growth forest in Congaree Swamp National Monument, South Carolina, USA: Canadian Journal of Forest Research, v. 21, p. 1765–1770.

Rikard, M., 1988, Hydrologic and vegetative relationships of the Congaree Swamp National Monument: Clemson, S.C., Clemson University, Ph.D. dissertation.

Quarterman, E., and Keever, K., 1962, Southern mixed hardwood forest—climax in the southeast coastal plain USA: Ecological Monographs, v. 32, p.167–185.

Sharitz, R.R., Vaitkus, M.R., and Cook, A.E., 1993, Hurricane damage to an old-growth flood plain forest in the Southeast, *in* Brissette, J.C., ed., Proceedings of the Seventh Southern Silvicultural Research Conference: U.S. Forest Service General Technical Report 50–53, p. 203–210.

Stahle, D.W., and Cleaveland, M.K., 1992, Reconstruction and analysis of spring rainfall over the Southeastern U.S. for the past 1000 years: Bulletin of the American Meteorological Society, v. 73, p. 1947–1961.

Stahle, D.W., and Cleaveland, M.K., 1994, Tree-ring reconstructed rainfall over the Southeastern USA during the Medieval warm period and Little Ice-Age: Climatic Change, v. 26, p. 199–212.

Stahle, D.W., Cleaveland, M.K., and Hehr, J.G., 1985, A 450-year drought reconstruction for Arkansas, United States: Nature, v. 316, p. 530–532.

Stahle, D.W., Cleaveland, M.K., and Hehr, J.G., 1988, North Carolina climate change reconstructed from tree rings— A.D. 372 to 1985: Science, v. 240, p. 1517–1519.

Stokes, M.A., and Smiley, T.L., 1964, An introduction to tree-ring dating: University of Chicago Press.

Thompson, A.J., 1998, An ecological inventory and classification of an old-growth flood plain forest in the Southeastern United States coastal plain: Athens, University of Georgia, M.S. thesis.

Ware, S., Frost, C., and Doerr, P., 1993, Southern mixed hardwood forest—the former longleaf pine forest region, *in* Martin, W.H., Boyce, S.A., and Echternacht, A.C., eds., Biodiversity of the Southeastern United States: New York, John Wiley and Sons, p. 447–493.

West, D.C., Doyle, T.W., Tharp, M.L., Beauchamp, J.L., Platt, W.J., and Downing, D.J., 1993, Recent growth increases in old-growth longleaf pine: Canadian Journal of Forest Research, v. 23, p. 846–853.

Wharton, C.H., Kitchens, W.M., Pendleton, E.C., and Sipe, T.W., 1982, The ecology of bottomland hardwood swamps of the Southeast—a community profile: U.S. Fish and Wildlife Service, FWS/OBS–81/37.

Whetstone, B.H., 1982, Techniques for estimating magnitude
and frequency of floods in South Carolina: U.S. Geological
Survey Water Resources Investigations 82–1.

Young, P.J., Keeland, B.D., and Sharitz, R.R., 1995, Growth
response of baldcypress to an altered hydrologic regime:
American Midland Naturalist, v. 133, p. 206–212.

Publishing support provided by
Lafayette Publishing Service Center

www.ingramcontent.com/pod-product-compliance
Lightning Source LLC
Chambersburg PA
CBHW080450290526
45791CB00008BA/2663